"A powerful and comprehensive guide to magickal protection that everyone should have by their side. Barbara Meiklejohn-Free has created a work that covers every aspect of spiritual and energetic defense—from the subtle to the sacred, the ancient to the modern."

—**LYNNE FRANKS**, OBE, founder of SEED Women's Empowerment Platform

PRAISE FOR *SHIELD. WARD. BIND & BANISH*

"This is the most practical and comprehensive guide to protective magick yet published. Grounded in experience and focused on real-world results, it offers effective techniques for virtually any situation accessible to anyone in need."

—**PROFESSOR RONALD HUTTON,** MA (Cantab.), DPhil (Oxon.), FRHistS, FSA., FLSW, FBA

"A fabulous in-depth book covering everything you need to know about working with protection magic from every level. A must-have for any magical practitioner, whether a beginner or more experienced."

—**RACHEL PATTERSON,** high priestess, podcast host, and bestselling author of over 30 books

"In a world veiled with unseen forces and energetic attack, Barbara Meiklejohn-Free emerges as a High Guardian of the Craft. With the clarity of a seer and the strength of a battle-tested witch, she guides readers through potent rituals, psychic defences, and soul-deep practices to reclaim their power, fortify their spirit, and walk fearlessly in both shadow and light."

—**FLAVIA KATE PETERS,** bestselling and award-winning author, high priestess, and fairy seer

"This beautifully written book is a quintessential guide to the power of protection, magick, and witchcraft. Threaded through every page, the ancient wisdom of our ancestors is stunningly captured in spells and practices that incorporate everything you could need in modern-day witchcraft.... There is nothing left out in this superb homage to ancestral power and elemental tradition."

—**NICKY ALAN,** bestselling author, psychic medium, and angel communicator

"This is a true companion for anyone walking a magickal path of protection—empowering, shielding, and deeply affirming. A guide to reclaim your energy, honour your boundaries, and walk forward in strength. It's more than a book—it's a remembering."
—**TJ HIGGINS**, *Sunday Times* bestselling author, mentor, podcaster, and radio host

"A lifetime of devotion, experience, and ancestral wisdom is masterfully woven into this essential guide to protection magick. Barbara Meiklejohn-Free has created more than just a book—she's gifted us a powerful companion for life. Written from the heart, every page pulses with practical tools, sacred insights, and daily guidance to shield your energy, space, and spirit."
—**LAURA O'ROURKE**, editor in chief of *Witches* magazine (Witches-Magazine.com)

"This is no ordinary book—it is a sacred talisman, a grimoire of protection woven from threads of ancient magick and lived wisdom. In these turbulent times, Barbara Meiklejohn-Free offers not only tools of defence, but keys to remembrance. Her words speak directly to the soul."
—**GORDON SMITH**, international medium, teacher, and bestselling author of over 15 books

"Barbara Meiklejohn-Free is a true elder of the path—grounded, wise, and deeply rooted in the old ways. *Shield, Ward, Bind & Banish* is the fruit of her lived experience in magical protection, shaped by her Highland heritage and decades of walking with seers and spirit teachers worldwide.... Barbara teaches that true protection is not born of fear but sovereignty, sacred boundaries, and the power of knowing who we are."
—**DAVID WELLS**, past-life and psychic protection expert and bestselling author

SHIELD, WARD, BIND & BANISH

ABOUT THE AUTHOR

Barbara Meiklejohn-Free, known as The Highland Seer, was born in the Highlands of Scotland and raised within a lineage of hereditary witches. Guided by her Auntie Barbara from Caithness, the renowned Highland Seer Swein Macdonald, and her grandmother Winnie, she was taught the ancient ways of traditional Scottish witchcraft—a living craft rooted in seership, the land, and ancestral remembrance.

An international bestselling and award-winning author, Barbara is recognised worldwide as a hereditary witch, shaman, medium, and transmedium, as well as a wisdom keeper and teacher of the old ways. For more than five decades, she has shared her craft through ritual, ceremony, and storytelling—rekindling the power of earth-based magick for modern times.

She is the author of over fifteen oracle decks and ten books and diaries published globally and the founder of the Coven of Arnemetia. Barbara offers a range of online teachings, including Year-and-a-Day Witchcraft Initiations to Third Degree, Death Doula Training, Magickal Protection, and Shamanic Practitioner and Teacher courses.

She is also a regular columnist for *Witchcraft and Wicca* magazine and *The Witch Magazine*. She contributes to several other well-known publications throughout the UK, where she shares insights on witchcraft, shamanism, and spiritual wisdom.

Through her Spirit Visions teachings, Barbara continues to share Scottish folk magick, seer-craft, and shamanic wisdom, guiding others to reclaim their authentic power and walk the path of remembrance.

SHIELD, WARD, BIND & BANISH

A WITCH'S GUIDE TO MAGICKAL PROTECTION

BARBARA MEIKLEJOHN-FREE

WOODBURY, MINNESOTA

FIRST EDITION
First Printing, 2026

Book design by Christine Ha
Cover design by Shannon McKuhen
Interior illustrations by the Llewellyn Art Department

Library of Congress Cataloging-in-Publication Data (Pending)
ISBN: 978-0-7387-6609-6

Llewellyn Publications
A Division of Llewellyn Worldwide Ltd.
2143 Wooddale Drive
Woodbury, MN 55125-2989
www.llewellyn.com

Printed in the United States of America

GPSR Representation:
UPI-2M PLUS d.o.o., Medulićeva 20, 10000 Zagreb, Croatia,
matt.parsons@upi2mbooks.hr

OTHER BOOKS BY BARBARA MEIKLEJOHN-FREE

Divination of the Ancients

Shamanic Medicine Oracle Cards

Witches' Wisdom Oracle Cards

Dark Goddess Oracle Cards

Witches' Kitchen Oracle Cards

Scottish Witchcraft

Witches' Familiars Oracle Cards

Witches' Moon Magick Oracle

Witches of the Craft Oracle Cards

CONTENTS

Introduction
A WHISPER FROM THE THORNS

There was a time when the veil between the world we perceive around us and the unseen realm was so thin that the forces of light and shadow danced openly. Our distant ancestors knew that the world was not simply what lay before their eyes but was interwoven with energies, spirits, and powers as old as the land they walked upon. As a result, they actively protected themselves. They warded their homes, carried amulets, cast sigils, and invoked the powers of the elements. They respected these energies and understood the necessity of guarding against them.

However, with the rise of monotheistic religions, particularly Christianity, the sacred practices were cast into shadow. The Church sought to unify spiritual power under a single divine source, and anything outside this doctrine was deemed heretical. The powerful charms and rituals that had once protected homes, children, and communities were labelled dangerous, and those who practised them were cast out, feared, or persecuted. The wise folk who had once held the knowledge of protection spells were hunted as witches, their wisdom forced into silence under the weight of religious persecution.

Today, many people move through life oblivious to the energies swirling around them. Only now, with the loss of ancestral wisdom, have we become exposed, vulnerable, and blind to the currents of energy that affect our health, minds, and spirits. In our modern world, we have grown so far from the traditions of our ancestors that we've forgotten the importance of magickal protection. The forces of darkness, envy, fear, and malice have not disappeared. They remain as potent today as they were thousands of years ago. Many people believe that protection is no longer necessary and that traditional methods have no place in a world of science and technology. But this couldn't be farther from the truth.

Every day, you are surrounded by energies, from the people you encounter to the spaces you move through. Invisible forces brush against you, some nourishing, others draining. Our forebearers lived with a heightened awareness, understanding that safeguarding one's energy wasn't a luxury but a necessity. So, they invoked their protection spells, mitigating any harm or ill intention.

Why have we forgotten this? Why do so many people move through life as if the unseen world has no influence? Could it be that we have come to believe science holds all the answers while the rest is mere mumbo jumbo? Some might argue that we don't need woo-woo when we possess rationality. Perhaps the information or knowledge we once held and shared has been discarded or purposefully hidden. The art of magickal protection, once an integral part of daily life, has faded from our modern consciousness. And now, more than ever, it's time to reawaken that wisdom.

A LIFE OF MAGICK

The following book wasn't something I sat down and planned. It has been whispering to me since childhood, growing inside of me with every step, ritual, and time I felt that shiver of knowing when something unseen had entered my sacred space, saying, "You must write this." And now, here it is, not just a book but a living testament to the journey I've walked with magickal protection my entire life.

As early as I remember, protection was never just about physical safety. It was something more profound, spiritual, energetic, magickal. It was a way of life.

In my family, the art of protection was handed down like recipes, etched in memory, stirred by instinct, and waiting not to be read from a book, but to be spelt into being. It was instinctive, inherited, alive. Grandmother Winnie taught me to speak to herbs, sense when something was off, and call in energies to guard my energy and space. Aunty Barbara was the kind of hedgewitch who worked with the magickal properties of blackthorn and hawthorn, who didn't just protect—they warded and shielded. She showed me that boundaries can be beautiful and fierce within the craft of the wise, as it was known then.

Then there was my dad, his silence, his deep knowing. He spoke little about such things, but when Queenie, the Traveller Witch, came to the door and talked to him about charms and Highland folklore, I watched. I listened. I remembered. She wasn't just a visitor but a signpost, a spirit of the old ways, guiding me back to the spirit within every living being, be it root, tree, or herbs. I was mesmerised by the old stories and always wanted more.

I was born in the Highlands of Scotland, where the winds are wild and the land feels sentient. That place shaped me and taught me to listen to the stones, the spaces between, and the spirits that linger in the corners. And as I grew older, I felt the pull to go farther—not to escape, but to deepen. My soul called me to other lands: the deserts of Egypt, the temples of South America, the vast plains of North America, the red earth of Australia. And in every place, ceremony, teaching, ritual, and rite of passage, I noticed one common thread: Magickal protection was always present in my day-to-day life.

It wasn't always named, and it didn't always look like a spell or circle. But it was there, in the chants, oils, dances, silence, weaving, and watching. It was in the way sacred people carried themselves. It was in the way they guarded what mattered to them as well as the spirits of power and place.

And so this book was born, not just from my mind, but from my life—from over sixty years of working with energy, spirit, and the unseen forces that shape our lives. This book comes from the people I've helped who didn't even realise they were under attack from spirits, from others, from their leaking energy. It's written for the empaths who can't sleep; the witches who feel drained after a simple conversation; the intuitive souls who've never been taught to shield, ward, bind, and banish; and the everyday people who wonder why their home never feels quite settled.

RECLAIMING MAGICKAL PROTECTION

As the world grows more chaotic, the energies of negativity, manipulation, and spiritual attack are seeping into our lives. The effects are real: illness, anxiety, unexplained misfortunes, and a feeling of heaviness that lingers no matter what we do.

People are losing their way, consumed by the energies they don't even realise they're absorbing. The energy surrounding us is as real today as it was for our ancestors. Nefarious forces, psychic attacks, envy, and malice are not distant threats; they are woven into the very fabric of our world. But as magickal beings, we have the power to defend ourselves, to stand strong in our light, and to cast away those energies that seek to harm or drain us.

Woven throughout the pages of this book are sacred pillars of magickal protection: shielding, warding, binding, and banishing. They form the roots of this work, but they are not its entirety. Around them spiral many other abilities, rites, and ancestral tools, all crafted to help you stand firm in your power and be protected in your path.

Let this book be a guide to help you reclaim your power. You will discover the tools and wisdom of the ancients, adapted for the modern world. You will learn to protect yourself from harmful energies, cleanse your space, and create powerful wards to safeguard your mind, body, and spirit. As you walk this path, you will become more aware of the energies surrounding you. You will learn to defend your spirit, home, and loved ones from the forces seeking harm. Most importantly, you will rediscover the magick within yourself—the power to protect, shield, and thrive—no matter what energies may come your way.

Each chapter is a path, a ritual, a spell in itself. Together, they create a full circle of defence or a shield, so your energy remains yours and yours alone.

You'll find spells, rituals, and daily practices passed to me through those who taught not by book, but by breath. Swein Macdonald, the Highland Seer, showed me the power of rooted, land-based protection. Ralph Harvey, alongside his wife, Audrey, initiated me as a High Priestess of Isis and taught me psychic shielding that still stands strong today. Abdul Mohamed, a Kemetic mystic, shared the ancient ways of oils, herbs, and resins, where magickal protection is worn like a second skin. So many others walked beside me, toward the destination of completing this book, and now their wisdom walks beside you.

I cannot stress this enough: Magickal protection is not a chore. It is sacred. It is daily. It is your birthright. When you weave it into your life, it will change everything. You'll feel stronger. Clearer. More empowered and free.

Let this book be your companion, guide, and magickal protection handbook. Let it remind you that you are never powerless. You were born with the ability to shield, defend, banish what does not serve, and walk as a sovereign being through every shadowed corner of this world.

Part One
GETTING STARTED

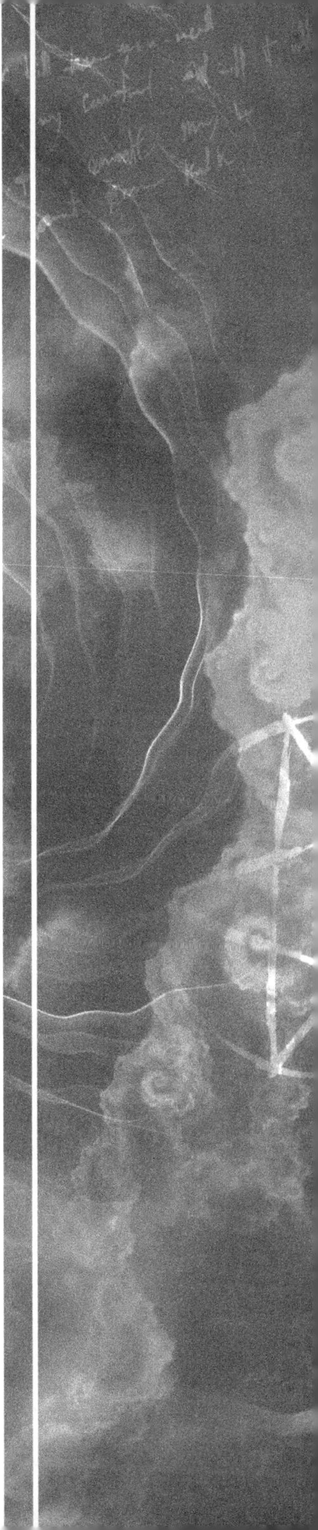

1
WHAT IS MAGICKAL PROTECTION?

Using magickal protection, also known as protection magick, shields against energies, opposing forces, and spiritual attacks. This practice stretches back through the ages, with roots in many ancient cultures where the first wardings and protective symbols were etched into stone, woven into spells, and embodied in the sacred rituals of the priesthood.

From the protective amulets of the ancient Egyptian pharaohs to the wards placed on tombs, safeguarding one's spirit from harm was paramount. But what, exactly, is magickal protection? It protects your spirit, mind, and aura beyond physical safety and integrity. It shields the witch from psychic attacks, spiritual intrusions, curses, and the energies of others that may cause harm.

TYPES OF PROTECTION

This protection can be summoned through spells, charms, sigils, and rituals, allowing us to harness the elemental forces to stand firm against the shadows that move through the world. Protecting ourselves (body, mind, and spirit) encompasses many methods. Therefore, it's essential to understand the nuances between our different forms of protection. Let's explore how arcane, psychic, personal, and energetic protections differ and how they weave together in our practice.

ARCANE PROTECTION

Arcane protection uses spells, enchantments, and rituals to ward off harmful forces. It is an intentional act of weaving protection into one's life, using the power of the elements, symbols, and ancient wisdom to create strong barriers between ourselves and those energies that seek to drain or harm us. Arcane protection can take many forms, but these are the most common:

- Warding spells create energetic barriers around your home, sacred space, or body.
- Protective charms, such as talismans, shield against curses, negative spirits, or ill will.
- Ritual cleansing removes unwanted energy or attachments through the use of smoke, salt, and water.
- Sigils are personally crafted symbols used to invoke protective energies. To create a sigil, write your intention, such as, "I am protected from harm." Then, remove the vowels and any repeating letters, leaving you with consonants. Use these remaining letters to form a symbol that feels magickal to you. This sigil now carries your intention and can be used to amplify your protection.
- Symbols. You can also work with traditional symbols, such as the pentacle, the triskelion, the Eye of Horus, or protective runes, incorporating them into your craft in meaningful ways. Whether drawing

them on parchment, engraving them into tools, or wearing them as jewellery, symbols are a powerful link between your energy and the protective forces you call upon.

PSYCHIC PROTECTION

Whilst similar to arcane protection, psychic protection shields the mind and soul from psychic attacks and negative thought-forms. These attacks can come from others, either consciously or unconsciously, or from negative entities that seek to drain your mental and emotional energy. Psychic protection is about creating mental and spiritual barriers to prevent these energies from taking hold. Barriers and methods include these:

- Psychic shields are employed by visualising a protective shield around your aura that deflects negative energy and psychic intrusion.
- Mental fortification strengthens your mind and emotional core through meditation, mantras, or breathwork.
- Banishing negative thoughtforms, actively cleansing your space and mind of harmful thoughts or energies projected by others.

PERSONAL PROTECTION

Personal protection is the defence of the self, body, mind, and spirit against both mundane and spiritual harm. It incorporates arcane and psychic protection elements but focuses on grounding and reinforcing our physical safety and emotional well-being. It's also about maintaining firm emotional and physical boundaries that prevent others from draining or manipulating our energy. These techniques include:

- Physical talismans, wearing enchanted jewellery or carrying objects charged with protective energy.
- Boundary setting involves establishing firm personal boundaries in relationships to prevent emotional manipulation or harm.
- Daily protection rituals invoke protective deities, spirits, or ancestors for personal safety throughout the day.

ENERGETIC PROTECTION

Energetic protection shields your life force, also known as your aura or chi, from depletion or intrusion by external energies. It is about maintaining the integrity of your energy field, ensuring that it remains clear, strong, and impenetrable by unwanted influences. Energetic protection involves working directly with your aura and the energy centres of your body to keep them balanced and resilient. Methods include:

- Aura cleansing. Use herbal smoking sticks, bells, or crystals to cleanse and fortify your energy field.
- Energy shields. Visualise a bubble of energy around you that absorbs or deflects negative vibrations.
- Chakra protection. Ensure your energy centres (chakras) are clear, aligned, and protected from external disruption.

ETHICAL CONSIDERATIONS

Protection magick, while powerful, has ethical considerations. We are called to act with intention, integrity, and respect for the energies with which we work. Protection spells and rituals should be grounded in the desire to shield ourselves or others from harm without causing unnecessary harm or manipulation. One critical ethical consideration is the law of balance, which ensures that when we protect ourselves, we do not inadvertently harm others. For example, casting a protection spell to shield yourself from negative influences is a responsible action.

However, spells that manipulate others or interfere with their free will, even under protection, can create unintended consequences and energetic imbalances. It's also important to reflect on the intention behind the spell. Are you acting out of fear, anger, or revenge, or are you genuinely seeking to create a safe and protected space? Protection magick should always be rooted in the intent to maintain peace, not to escalate conflicts or generate more chaos.

Last, when performing protection rituals, crafting spells, or other magickal practices for others, always seek their consent. While it may feel natural to want to protect a loved one, ensuring they are open to receiving the protection is crucial. Unwanted magick, even with good intentions, can disrupt the recipient's energy and autonomy.

WHEN NOT TO PERFORM RITUALS OR SPELLS

There are times when it is not a good idea to perform rituals or spells, as you may struggle to execute them properly, and the outcomes may not be what you desire, or may even be harmful or detrimental. Here is a list of such times.

- When you are physically ill, your body's energy is focused on healing, making it harder to concentrate on magick. Rest and recover before performing any rituals.
- When you feel emotionally drained. Emotional exhaustion scatters your energy, making it challenging to direct power effectively. Rejuvenate yourself first.
- When your heart isn't in it. Without passion or genuine focus, magick becomes weak. Wait until you feel fully aligned with the purpose of the ritual.
- When you're angry or agitated. Magick cast in anger carries chaotic energy, which can backfire. Calm yourself before proceeding with any spellwork.
- When you're feeling depressed. Low-vibrational states, like depression, can dilute the power of your magick. Take time to lift your spirits before working with energy.
- When you are spiritually disconnected. A lack of spiritual connection weakens your magick. Ground yourself and reconnect with your higher self before casting spells.
- When you're under the influence of substances. Alcohol or drugs cloud judgment and disrupt energy flow. Always work with magick while sober and clear-minded.
- When you are rushed or distracted. Rushed rituals lead to scattered, unfocused energy. Wait until you have the time and attention to devote yourself fully to the spell.

- When you are doubting your power. Self-doubt weakens your magick. Build confidence in your abilities before attempting any ritual.
- When you're feeling fearful or anxious. Fear distorts your energy and intention. Take time to ground yourself and release anxiety before casting any spells.
- When you're performing for ego or personal gain. Magick rooted in ego or selfish motives disrupts the balance.

Approaching protection magick with clarity, respect, and a deep understanding of its potential effects ensures you work in harmony with universal energies, creating robust and ethically sound protection.

2

THE FOUNDATIONS OF PROTECTION

The strength of our magick lies not just in the rituals we perform but in the protective foundations we establish. Mastering the wards, charms, and enchantments lays a secure foundation for your magickal practice. You are fortifying your space, your tools, and your spirit. The tools, poppets, and spell jars we will create are more than just physical objects—they are extensions of our energy, intention, and personal power. To craft them safely and effectively, we must first ensure that we are protected, grounded, and shielded from harmful influences.

These practices are protective measures and pillars upon which all future magick is built. Without setting proper wards or invoking protective symbols, we leave ourselves vulnerable to interference from unseen forces, negative energies, or even our unfocused intent. Protection is not an afterthought; it is the armour we wear as we enter the sacred space of witchcraft.

THE POWER OF INTENTION

In the world of magick, it's easy to become lost in elaborate tools, lengthy rituals, and intricate spells. But at the heart of every act of protection lies a single truth: Intention is everything. A witch who pours their focused will into a ritual for two minutes will have done more powerful work than someone who spends two hours casting without intention. It is not the length of time nor the number of ingredients but the clarity of your mind and the strength of your desire that fuels the spell.

As you begin practising the rituals and spells of magickal protection in your daily life, remember that intention is everything. Set your intention with purpose, clarity, and conviction. Always ensure your intentions are pure and aligned with your higher purpose. Know that your protection is already forming when you set your intention; the ritual is how you manifest that power into being.

Picture this: As you craft a charm bag for protection, you carefully select each herb and crystal—black tourmaline for grounding, rosemary (*Salvia rosmarinus*) for cleansing, and a personal item for connection. Yet, it is not these items alone that protect. You must whisper your intention into the spell, calling forth the energies to weave together and form a potent charm. With each word and gesture, your will shapes the magick, forming an impenetrable barrier of protection.

When your intention is aligned, you become the conduit for magickal energy. In those moments, the work is done. Whether it's a whispered charm, quick sigils drawn on your skin, or a single word spoken with purpose, the intention seals the magick. I always say, "As you think, so it shall be."

Protection magick is not passive magick, but a dance between you and the energies you summon. The symbols and objects serve as your allies, but your intention, steady as a flame in the dark, directs the power, weaving the spell into the fabric of the universe. When your heart and mind are aligned, when your intention is clear and fierce, your magick becomes an unbreakable fortress, standing strong against all harm.

THE ENCHANTMENT OF POSITIVITY

When the veil thins and we stand at the crossroads of magick, where arcane allies and ancient energies await, we must anchor ourselves in the strength of focus and the ardency of positivity. The path ahead may glitter with possibility, yet it also hums with powerful, unseen forces. To walk this road confidently, we must guard our spirit, ensuring that we remain grounded in the light of intention.

Focus sharpens our magickal sight, allowing us to see beyond the mundane and into the sacred realms. But without it, we risk becoming untethered, adrift in the waves of energies that are not our own. Positivity, like the steady flame of a lantern, illuminates our way and aligns us with the higher vibrations that arcane allies naturally gravitate toward. Through this focus, bathed in the light of positivity, we can engage with these forces and remain empowered in their presence.

Remember, the work we do is profound and transformative. We call upon energies older than time with every spell and invocation, yet we must first prepare our energetic bodies to wield them safely. To remain positive is to protect your power. To stay focused is to harness it with precision. Together, these form the foundation upon which all magickal workings are built.

In the world of witches, positivity isn't just a state of mind; it's a potent force that weaves its way through our spells, rituals, and daily lives. Like the shimmer of moonlight on a dark path, maintaining positive energy protects against negativity, malevolent forces, and unwanted influences.

The individual who carries positivity is like a beacon, shining brightly against the shadows. This isn't about superficial happiness, but rather a deep-rooted inner strength that radiates into the world. When our spirits are high and our thoughts aligned with light, we naturally repel those forces that seek to disrupt, drain, or harm us.

Our ancestral wise folk knew positivity could cast an invisible circle of protection, forming a barrier that darker entities and energies could not penetrate. Here, we blend the subtle art of positivity with magick, infusing our spells, spaces, and selves with a vibrant energy that keeps negativity at bay. A list of the fundamental magickal ways to cultivate positivity for protection follows:

- ***Affirmations as incantations.*** Words hold power, and when spoken with intention, they become magick. Affirmations are akin to ancient incantations; when spoken daily, they cast an energetic circle around us, empowering our spirit and protecting us from harm. If you take just one protection affirmation from this book, you would be hard-pressed to find one more effective than saying, "I walk in the light of protection; no harm may enter my space. Only love surrounds me by the will of the god and goddess, and darkness cannot remain. I am cloaked in a veil of joy; no shadow may touch my heart."

- *Gratitude charm.* Gratitude has long been revered as a powerful charm for protection and well-being. The energy of thankfulness resonates at the highest frequency, warding off jealousy, envy, and ill will. A witch who embraces gratitude walks with an unseen shield, shimmering in the light of their blessings.
- *Gratitude ritual.* Light a silver candle under the moon's glow and place a small crystal, such as clear quartz or moonstone, at the centre of your altar. Whisper words of gratitude, offering thanks for the blessings that have come your way: "By the light of the stars, I give thanks to the spirits who guard and guide me. I am blessed, I am shielded, I am protected by the love that surrounds me." Allow the candle to burn as you bask in the protective energy of gratitude.

Spell: Uplifting Energy

By embracing the power of positivity in your magickal practice, you create a natural shield against darkness and ill will. This magick of light, laughter, and joy becomes an ongoing protection ritual, ensuring your energy remains pure, strong, and untouchable by negativity. Through the ancient art of maintaining a bright aura and positive spirit, you call upon the highest forces to stand with you, creating a circle of radiant protection in all you do. You can use colours like white, yellow, and gold to brighten your home and add crystals like citrine or sunstone to amplify your personal energy.

Needs

A golden cloth to cover your altar or table, a bright taper candle (e.g., yellow, white, or gold), a candleholder, fresh flowers symbolising joy (such as sunflowers [*Helianthus annuus*] or daisies [*Bellis perennis*]), and a vase with water for the flowers.

Directions

Decorate your altar or tabletop with the cloth, flowers in the vase, and the candle. Light a candle and say: "By this light, I call forth joy, peace, and protection. May this space shine with love, and may my spirit be uplifted." Let the candle burn until it's out, filling the room with warmth and positive energy.

Do not leave the candle unattended. If you must leave the space, put the candle out and relight it when you return.

ECHOES OF THE EGYPTIANS

There comes a time in life when the veil between worlds becomes so thin that it beckons us to reclaim the ancient knowledge lost to time. For me, that time came when I stood in Luxor, Egypt, amidst the sanctuaries of ancient wisdom. The stones of the Karnak Temple whispered tales of epochs long past, and I walked with the familiarity of a soul returning home.

The curious gaze of Egyptologists has always mirrored the questions that danced within my spirit, but the land knew I had come for something more profound. Ancient Egyptians were the keepers of powerful magick, crafting spells and rituals to protect their temples, homes, and spirits from the forces lurking in the seen and unseen worlds.

It was here, within the hallowed halls of Karnak, that the veil lifted for me, revealing the sacred dance of past lives intertwined with the present. It is no coincidence that I returned to the places of power, where magick flows like the Nile, ever winding and eternal. For me, Egypt holds the keys to unlocking magickal protection, an art deeply woven into their everyday lives, where they blended ritual, medicine, and magick as seamlessly as the sun rises and sets.

HEKA AND THE SACRED POWER OF MAGICK

Heka is the Ancient Egyptian god of magick and medicine, as well as a word used to mean "magick." Heka embodies the life force that animates all things, the spark of creation that runs through the cosmos, gods, and mortals alike. He was thought to be the force that allowed the gods to perform miracles, enact healing, and protect the world from chaos.

We call upon Heka today because he embodies the ancient thread of magick that connects the realms of spirit, body, and the unseen energies that shape our world. By invoking his name, we tap into the same wellspring of power used by ancient Egyptians to create, destroy, and renew. When we call upon Heka, we summon protection for the body, spirit, and mind, bringing balance between the seen and unseen worlds. His power ensures that our rituals are not mere actions but the manifestation of deep, transformative magick.

WORKING WITH HEKA

Incorporating Heka into our modern-day practice enables us to tap into the past, drawing forth the ancient art of protection, healing, and spiritual defence. We blend ancient Egyptian wisdom with contemporary needs, invoking the primal energies of the earth and cosmos to guard ourselves and those we love. One of the most effective ways to incorporate Heka into contemporary practice is by integrating magickal practices with modern medicine, much like the ancient Egyptians did.

You might use Heka's energy to empower the healing process if you undergo medical treatment. This can be as simple as placing a protective symbol over a prescribed medicine or saying a prayer to Heka before taking it, asking for his protection and for the medicine to work in alignment with your highest good.

Heka was also invoked through the natural elements of fire, earth, water, and air. You can connect to the elemental forces in your rituals to draw Heka's protective energy into your sacred space. Whether lighting a candle to represent the fire of creation, pouring water to bless and purify your body and soul, or standing barefoot on the earth to ground and centre yourself, Heka's ancient magick flows through these natural forces. You weave the ancient into your modern-day practice through these connections, creating a bridge between worlds, the past and the present.

Ritual: Invocation of Heka

You can perform this simple ritual to call upon Heka in magickal workings, whether for protection, healing, or spiritual empowerment. This rite honours the ancient ways while grounding the practice in the present.

Through this invocation, you summon the ancient force of Heka, blending the wisdom of magick and medicine into your life and calling forth the protective energy that flows through time and space. Whether used for healing or spiritual defence, Heka's presence reinforces the bonds between the physical and the magickal, reminding us that true protection is not just about shielding the body but also about fortifying the spirit and soul.

Needs

A gold or yellow taper candle (symbolising the sun and divine energy), a vessel of Nile water or fresh river water imbued with Egyptian oils, a piece of lapis lazuli, frankincense (*Boswellia sacra*) or sandalwood (*Santalum album*), and a quiet space.

Directions

Light the incense and allow the scent to fill your space. Place the candle before you and the vessel of water beside it. Ground yourself, feeling the ancient energies beneath your feet. Then stand tall and call upon the elements to join you in your work by saying, "By fire's light and earth's foundation, by wind's breath and water's salvation, I call forth the magick in me; Heka, come forth and set me free."

Next light the candle and say, "Heka, God of Magick, I summon thee, through time and space, come forth to me. By the power of the gods and the magick you weave, guard my soul and let me believe. In healing's light and protection's shield, your ancient strength, let now be revealed. I call you forth, great power of old, through this magick, I shall be bold."

Now empower the water by holding your hands over the water vessel and imagine Heka's ancient power flowing through you. Visualise the water filling with light, becoming a conduit for healing and protection and say, "The water of life, blessed by Heka's hand, heal, protect, by ancient command. With every drop, let magick flow, through body, spirit, and heart below."

Next, seal the magick by holding the stone in your hand, focusing your energy on it, and saying, "This stone now holds protection's grace charged by Heka through time and space. Guard me now, with power divine, shield and heal, O magick of mine." Place the stone on your altar, if you have one, or carry it for ongoing protection. Finally, complete the ritual by snuffing out the candle and saying, "By Heka's power and divine decree, I am healed, I am shielded, so mote it be."

GUARDIANS OF THE SACRED FLAME

In the shadows of ancient temples, where the sacred fires burned, and the whispers of the gods filled the air, I imagine the temple priests and priestesses of Egypt weaving rituals that carried the weight of the cosmos and blending sacred rites with the power of the elements. They called upon the divine forces to guard their people, their homes, and their lands against unseen threats. They did not simply call upon the gods; they channelled the raw magick that flowed through the veins of creation itself.

I envision these temple priests as guardians of sacred knowledge and the architects of powerful protective magick. Their prayers were not merely prayers but invocations of the divine power that could turn away ill fortune, drive out malicious spirits, and safeguard the soul.

For witches today, the ancient priesthood offers a wealth of knowledge long buried beneath the sands of time. Their rituals were intricate, balancing the elements, invoking celestial powers, and weaving magick with such clarity that the forces they summoned could be felt in every breath of wind and flicker of flame. These rites remind us that protection is more than just a spell; it is a sacred duty, a bond between the witch and the universe.

Studying these ancient practices teaches that protection goes beyond simply warding off negativity. It is about creating a sacred space, a temple within and without, where our energy is guarded, our boundaries are strong, and our connection to the divine is unbroken. By embracing these teachings, we tap into a magick older than time. We become the keepers of the ancient flame of Heka or magick, drawing upon the rituals of old to craft protection that is not just powerful but timeless.

3
THE ELEMENTS: YOUR INNER ARMOUR

When you harness the four elements within—air through your breath, fire through your will, water through your emotions, and earth through your grounding—you create a powerful, impenetrable shield around yourself. This shield becomes your inner armour, a reflection of the ancient wisdom that protected witches and mystics for centuries. With every breath, every intention, and every grounded step, you carry a layer of spiritual protection that transcends physical barriers. It is woven from the elements themselves, a sacred force that shields you from external harm and fortifies your spirit, strengthening your magick and amplifying your personal power.

OF LIFE AND MAGICK

The elements mirror the greater forces of the universe, which also flow within you, acting as your first line of magickal defence. Whether you are facing psychic attacks, negative energies, or the harshness of the modern world, your inner connection to the elements of air, fire, water, and earth allows you to stand strong, calm, and empowered before any spell is cast, even before any ward is set or protective charm is worn. To truly master the art of personal protection, you must learn to harness this elemental power and bring it forth, beginning with the most vital force of all: your breath.

For many spiritual people, breathing is considered far more than just a mundane necessity for life; It is a sacred, magickal act. With every inhale, witches have called upon the power of the element of air, drawing in the unseen forces surrounding us. With every exhale, they released intention, transforming their breath into a conduit for their will. The breath is the gateway to inner magick; it stirs the magickal fire within, cools with the waters of emotion, grounds with the force of the earth, and spreads the magickal energy of air through every cell of your being.

WHAT THE ELEMENTS PROVIDE

By harnessing these elemental forces, you can create a protective environment that reflects the earth's natural balance and power. They are your compass points, each offering a different way to tap into and work your magick and sense the unseen.

AIR

The swift currents of air dispel negativity. Burn incense or hang feathers by windows and doorways to invite the wind's energy to purify and protect your space. Hold a feather and allow it to drift through the area. A sudden shift without a breeze indicates energy is shifting.

FIRE

Fire purifies and destroys harmful forces. Lighting a candle creates a fiery boundary that keeps ill intentions from crossing your threshold. A simple tip to gauge the energy in a room (ensuring there are no apparent drafts) is to light a candle and observe the flame. A steady flame shows calm energy, while a flickering flame indicates the presence of unseen forces.

WATER

Water washes away negativity, purifying your space. Use blessed water or stormwater to anoint doors and windows, creating a fluid, ever-moving shield. Gaze into still water to reveal ripples of energy. A still surface means balance, while disturbances signal unrest.

EARTH

Earth's grounding force offers stability and strength. Stones like black hematite or salt placed around your space form a solid protective barrier, keeping harmful energies at bay. A quick and easy way to connect with this element is to put your hands on the ground and feel for vibrations. The earth will guide you and tell you if energies are harmonious or disturbed.

* * *

Now I will give you more detail about each element and the ways it helps build your inner armour.

THE BREATH OF LIFE: AIR

Air, the element of thought, inspiration, and movement, flows through you with every breath you take. Your breath is your power. It carries your intentions, desires, and protective magick into the world. Many witches have sat in sacred stillness, focusing solely on their breathing, until they could feel the power of the air element rising within them. This is where true magickal protection begins, within the rhythmic dance of breath.

When you breathe with intention, you are pulling the currents of the universe into your body, infusing your spirit with the wisdom of the winds, the whispers of your ancestors, and the clarity of thought. With every inhale, you draw in pure, protective energy from the air element. And with exhales, you release tension, fear, or negative energy that lingers within your aura. That is magick at work by itself.

Ritual: Witch's Breath

Give this short meditative ritual a try to work on your breathing power. As you master the art of breath, you align with the element of air within you, sharp, clear, and untouchable.

Needs

A quite space.

Directions

Sit quietly in your sacred space, close your eyes, and begin to breathe deeply. Inhale for a count of four, hold your breath for a moment, then exhale for a count of four. Visualise the air swirling around you like a gentle breeze. With each breath, feel your personal shield strengthen as you draw the protective energy of air into your body. Envision the air clearing away all lingering negativity, refreshing and renewing your energy.

THE SACRED FLAME WITHIN: FIRE

Breath alone is not enough to form your armour. To truly protect yourself, you must awaken the fire within, the sacred flame of your magickal soul. The fire element lives in your belly, your solar plexus, where your will and magickal drive burn brightest. When you call upon this inner fire, you ignite the protective force that burns away all negativity, doubt, and fear.

To strengthen your magickal protection, you must stoke the fire within. Feel its warmth growing as you breathe, merging with the air. Your breath fans the flames of your magick, awakening your inner power. This sacred fire burns bright within your chest, lighting up your aura and creating a radiant shield of protection that no ill intention can penetrate.

Meditation: Sacred Fire

Let the fire within you roar, for it is the very essence of your protective magick. Use this meditation to start that fire.

Needs

A quite space.

Directions

Place your hands over your solar plexus and take a deep breath, envisioning a golden flame flickering within your core. Feel the flame grow brighter and stronger with every breath, radiating warmth and protection outward. This flame is your magickal fire, your inner power. Envision this flame surrounding you, burning away any negative energy or psychic attacks lingering in your aura.

THE FLOW OF EMOTIONAL SHIELDING: WATER

Just as fire and air live within you, so too does water, the element of emotion, intuition, and healing. Water flows through your body, grounding you in the present and helping you stay fluid, adaptable, and in tune with the currents of the universe. While the fire burns away harmful energy, water cools and soothes, creating a gentle yet powerful protective barrier.

When the witches of old sought protection, they would often turn to the waters, sacred springs, moonlit rivers, or enchanted lakes, knowing that water could cleanse the body and the spirit. The same water flows through you now, a river of magick that connects you to your intuition and emotions. Honouring the water within allows your emotions to guide your magickal protections. You sense danger before it comes. You feel the flow of energy around you and adjust your shields accordingly.

Ritual: Water for Emotional Shielding

This ritual will help you feel a connection to the element of water. Like the ocean tides, your protection will flow and ebb as needed, keeping you safe.

Needs

A quite space.

Directions

Close your eyes and envision a cool, calming river flowing through your body. This river grows stronger with every breath, washing away any emotional clutter or fear that may cloud your protective shield. Feel the water within you strengthen your emotional defences, allowing you to remain calm and centred no matter what energies surround you.

GROUNDING POWER: EARTH

Finally, the element of earth, the most solid and steadfast of all, anchors your magickal protection. Earth is your foundation, the steady energy that grounds you in your power, keeping you centred and strong. Without the earth's grounding, your magickal shield would be like a leaf in the wind, quickly moved and vulnerable. But when you call upon the world within you, you root yourself deep, becoming as immovable as a mountain.

Take off your shoes. As you walk with bare feet, feel the ground's ancient power rise into you, rooting it to you and your magick. Feel the earth beneath you, its steady pulse anchoring your protection. Just as a tree's roots hold it fast in the face of storms, your connection to the element of the earth keeps your magickal protection grounded.

Ritual: Grounding

As you do the following ritual, feel yourself becoming solid, unshakeable, as the earth's energy merges with your breath, fire, and water.

Needs

A quite space outdoors, if possible.

Directions

Stand tall, with your feet firmly on the ground. Close your eyes and take a deep breath. As you exhale, imagine roots extending from your feet into the earth.

With each breath, feel these roots go deeper, grounding you and drawing up the strength of the earth. This grounding energy flows into your body, fortifying your magickal shield.

PENTACLE: THE SHIELD OF ELEMENTS

If you are looking to carry the protection of the elements with you in a simple yet effective way, the pentacle, a disc inscribed with a five-pointed star representing the elements, is a powerful protective symbol in witchcraft.

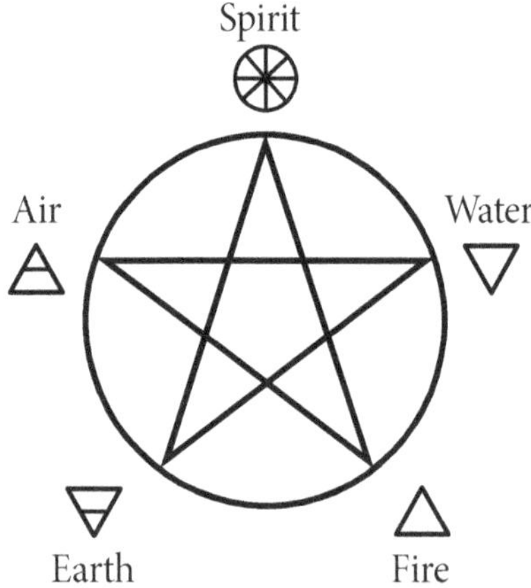

It acts as a shield and a conduit, calling on the elements to create a protective barrier. When placed on your altar or worn as a talisman, it strengthens your defences.

4

HARNESSING THE HEAVENS

Having examined the elements at work when it comes to magickal protection, we now look skyward to the celestial bodies that have a profound influence on all we do. To manage this in our protective practices, we associate each celestial body with a day of the week.

PLANETS AND THE DAYS

By aligning your rituals with each day's planetary energies, you ensure you are protected and empowered throughout the week, keeping you safe at all times, as described next.

MONDAY: THE MOON'S MYSTICAL SHIELD

The energy of the moon governs Mondays, making Monday an ideal time to focus on emotional and psychic protection. The moon's energy is fluid, intuitive, and deeply connected to the unseen, so this day is also ideal for creating a protective shield around your emotional and psychic self. The following invocation ensures that your emotions are shielded, allowing you to move through the day with a calm and clear mind.

To invoke this planet's power, light a silver or white candle and call upon the moon's gentle power to wrap your aura in a soft, shimmering shield of light. Say, "I shield my soul with the moon's glow; no harm may reach me, and no storm takes hold. My heart is guarded, and Luna protects my spirit light throughout the night."

TUESDAY: MARS'S FIERY FORTRESS OF DEFENCE

Mars, the planet of courage, strength, and protection, rules Tuesday. It's a day to focus on physical and energetic defence, empowering your body and spirit with Mars's fire. Carry red jasper or carnelian on Tuesday to stay connected to Mars's fiery strength, keeping your shields strong.

To invoke this planet's power, light a red candle and visualise a fierce fire surrounding you, burning away any negativity or harmful energy that may try to enter your space. Then say, "By Mars's flame, I cast this wall; no force may pass, and no ill may fall. My body is strong, my spirit true, and Mars protects me in all I do."

WEDNESDAY: MERCURY'S QUICK-WITTED DEFLECTION

Wednesday is governed by Mercury, the planet of communication and mental clarity. It's the perfect day to create mental shields that protect against confusion, manipulation, or harmful words. To amplify this mental protection, carry fluorite or agate, keeping your thoughts sharp and your energy shielded.

To invoke this planet's power, light a yellow candle and visualise Mercury's quicksilver energy wrapping around your mind in a bright, protective shield. Now say, "By Mercury's grace, my mind is clear, and I shall hold no harmful words near. My thoughts are bright, my speech is true, and Mercury's shield shall see me through."

THURSDAY: JUPITER'S GUARDIANSHIP OF BOUNDARIES

On Thursday, you align with the expansive energy of Jupiter, the planet of prosperity and abundance. It's a day to focus on protecting all you value, spiritually and materially. Place an amethyst or citrine on your altar to enhance Jupiter's protective and prosperous energy throughout the day.

To invoke this planet's power, light a purple candle and call upon Jupiter's energy to create a golden shield around your home, wealth, and personal power. Now say, "By Jupiter's power, I shield my worth; no harm shall touch, and no ill give birth. My bounty is safe, my spirit bright, and I am protected by Jupiter's might."

FRIDAY: VENUS'S LOVE-INFUSED PROTECTION

Venus, the planet of love and beauty, governs Friday. It's a time to focus on protecting your heart and relationships from negativity or discord. Rose quartz is a perfect crystal for Fridays, helping you maintain Venus's loving protection in your heart and your connections.

To invoke this planet's power, light a pink candle and call upon Venus to guard your heart with her loving, gentle energy. Now say, "By Venus's light, my heart is sealed; no harm may touch it, no pain revealed. My love is safe, my spirit strong; Venus protects me all day long."

SATURDAY: SATURN'S GUARDRAILS OF DISCIPLINE

Saturn's influence creates a solid foundation, substantial barriers, and unshakable defences. Born under this influence, I have always felt the need for strong protection, and I honour that power by performing extra protective rituals on Saturdays. I call upon Saturn's grounding energy on Saturdays to protect and secure my aura. Try keeping hematite or obsidian crystal on your person (held in your hand or pocket). Both stones are grounding and protective, to further align with this energy. Saturn's power flows through them, anchoring your shields and securing your magick.

To invoke this planet's power, light a black or dark blue candle, colours that resonate deeply with Saturn's steady, protective power. As the flame flickers, feel the energy of Saturn building a robust and impenetrable barrier around you, ensuring no harmful energy can pierce your sacred space. Once your space is secure, say, "By Saturn's ring, my shields are strong; no harm may touch me, and no ill belongs. My boundaries are firm, my spirit whole, and Saturn protects my body and soul."

SUNDAY: THE SUN'S RADIANCE FOR RECHARGING

Sunday is ruled by the sun, a day for recharging your spiritual energy and strengthening your aura. Sunstone or citrine helps you carry the sun's protective light throughout the day, keeping the spirit strong and radiant.

To invoke this planet's power, light a gold candle and stand in the sunlight, feeling its warmth and power flow through you, energising your spirit and restoring your shields. Now say, "By the sun's fire, my spirit is bright, protected by Sol's radiant light. No shadow may cross, no ill may remain, by the sun's power, I rise again."

HONOURING YOUR PLANETARY POWER

On the day you were born, you crossed through the veil, passing from the spirit world into the physical, guided by the planetary force that still protects and influences you. Setting up an altar specifically for your birthday is deeply important. This altar is a sacred reminder of the ascended planetary ruler that governs your path and the energies that shape your entrance into this world, and it serves as a tribute to that moment and is a powerful source of ongoing protection.

Keeping a permanent altar for your birthday ensures that all the necessary tools and magickal elements are readily available to strengthen your connection to your ruling planet. While you may incorporate other planetary influences into your practice, focusing on your birthday's altar is essential. If time does not allow for daily protection rituals, honouring your birthday alone will doubly ensure your protection throughout the week. The energy you harness today aligns with the core of who you are, reinforcing your shields and ensuring you are guarded all week long, even when daily protection isn't possible.

PLANETARY ALTARS

Setting up your altar in alignment with these celestial forces creates a powerful space for daily protection magick and personal empowerment. Following is a guide to crafting a witchy altar for the day of the week on which you were born, enhancing your connection to your planetary ruler and fortifying your shields. Each altar will require something that represents one of the governing colours, one of the gems or semiprecious stones, one of the items from the flora world, and items that invoke the energy and the main focus.

MONDAY'S MOON ALTAR

The moon altar governs emotional and psychic shielding and is associated with silver, white, and soft blue colours. Place a silver or white candle on the altar to honour the moon's light. Use moonstone, selenite, or pearl crystals for emotional clarity and psychic protection. Mugwort (*Artemisia vulgaris*), jasmine (*Jasminum officinale*), and lavender (*Lavandula angustifolia*) are said to enhance intuition and protect against nightmares. The crescent moon symbolises lunar energy. The focus is on emotional healing, psychic shielding, and dream protection.

TUESDAY'S MARS ALTAR

The altar for Mars governs physical and energetic defence and is associated with red, orange, and fiery tones. Place red or orange candles on the altar to honour Mars's fierce, protective fire; red jasper, carnelian, or bloodstone for strength and defence. Basil (*Ocimum basilicum*), ginger (*Zingiber officinale*), and nettle (*Urtica dioica*) for courage and protection. A sword or flame representation to invoke Mars's warrior spirit. Focus is on physical and energetic protection, courage, and grounding.

WEDNESDAY'S MERCURY ALTAR

For mental clarity and communication, create the Mercury altar, which is associated with yellow, light green, and shades of silver. Place a yellow candle on the altar to honour Mercury's quicksilver energy. Fluorite, agate, or citrine for mental clarity and focus. Peppermint (*Mentha × piperita*), lavender, and lemongrass (*Cymbopogon citratus*) to sharpen the mind. A feather or quill represents clear communication. Focus is on mental clarity, protection from gossip, and communication barriers.

THURSDAY'S JUPITER ALTAR

The Jupiter altar governs prosperity and boundary protection and is associated with royal blue, purple, and gold. Place a purple or royal blue candle on the altar to honour Jupiter's expansive and protective energy. Add amethyst, citrine, or lapis lazuli for abundance and spiritual defence along with common sage (*Salvia officinalis*), cinnamon (*Cinnamomum verum*), and dandelion (*Taraxacum officinale*) for prosperity and protection. A gold coin or key symbolises unlocked potential and wealth, and the focus is on guarding abundance, protecting boundaries, and spiritual growth.

FRIDAY'S VENUS ALTAR

The Venus altar governs heart protection and love and is associated with pink, green, and soft whites. Place a pink or green candle on the altar to channel Venus's love and beauty. Add rose quartz, emerald, or jade for heart protection and harmony. Rose petals (any species, preferably red or pink), hibiscus (*Hibiscus sabdariffa*), and thyme (*Thymus vulgaris*) for love, peace, and protection. A rose or heart symbol invokes love's protective power. Focus is on protecting love, relationships, and emotional balance.

SATURDAY'S SATURN ALTAR

Saturday's Saturn altar governs strong boundaries and grounding and is associated with black, dark blue, and deep earthy tones. Place a black or dark blue candle on the altar to honour Saturn's grounding and protective energy. Add hematite, obsidian, or onyx for boundary setting and protection. Cypress (*Cupressus sempervirens*), common sage, and comfrey (*Symphytum officinale*) to strengthen shields and boundaries. A ring or stone circle to represent Saturn's unbreakable shield. Focus on firm boundaries, grounding, and deep protection.

SUNDAY'S SUN ALTAR

The sun altar governs spiritual recharging and protection and is associated with gold, yellow, and orange. Place a gold or yellow candle on the altar to channel the sun's radiant energy. Sunstone, citrine, or clear quartz for spiritual strength and vitality. Bay leaves (*Laurus nobilis*), chamomile (*Chamaemelum nobile*), and calendula (*Calendula officinalis*) for protection and energy renewal. A sun emblem or solar wheel to invoke the power of the sun. Focus on spiritual protection, recharging personal power, and vitality.

Ritual: Sunrise Invocation

The following simple ritual will show you how to call on the sun's power on Sunday or any day.

Needs

A quiet space.

Directions

Open your arms to its golden light when the sun touches the sky. Speak words of power to greet the day, invoking the sun's energy as a radiant shield around you. Feel its warmth fill your aura, burning away negativity and illuminating your path. Recite a simple invocation like, "By the light of the dawn, I call forth magickal protection. As the sun rises, so shall my shield of light, guarding me until the sun sets."

HONOURING YOUR BIRTHDAY

I always emphasise that the day of your birth is a power day, a portal of magick and spiritual strength. The energies on this day are potent, and you are more connected to your planetary ruler than at any other time. It's essential to take the time to honour this powerful energy through a birthday ritual that weaves together protection, empowerment, and renewal. As you approach your birthday, the veil between the worlds seems thinner, and your connection to the cosmos is stronger.

This is not just a celebration of another year but a sacred moment where your personal power reaches its peak, and the universe aligns with the energy of your birth. On this day, you have a rare opportunity to call forth deeper protection and empower yourself in ways that resonate with the core of your soul.

Ritual: Birthday Protection

Following is the ritual I perform each year to ensure I am fully guarded and in alignment with the cosmic forces that support me. This ritual combines candles, crystals, herbs, and pure intention, spoken from my heart, to fortify my spirit and celebrate the journey ahead. By performing this ritual each year, you strengthen your connection to the powerful energies that align with your birth, fortifying your shields and ensuring that your life's journey remains protected. The day of your birth is a day of cosmic power, a time to reflect on your path and prepare for the road ahead, always walking with protection, purpose, and magick.

Needs

A candle aligned with your birthday's planet, a hematite, an obsidian, and an amethyst for grounding and protection. Dried rosemary, dried common sage, and dried mugwort for clearing and shielding. A bowl of spring or natural water to represent the cleansing flow of the spirit, a piece of paper and a pen for your intentions, and a small mirror for reflection and protection.

Directions

Find a quiet space where you can set up your permanent altar. Arrange your candle, crystals, herbs, and water. Cast a protective circle around you, calling on the spirits, ancestors, and planetary forces that align with your birthday. As you stand in this space, feel the energy of the cosmos swirling around you, strengthening your spirit.

Next, light the candle that represents the planetary ruler of your birthday. As the flame flickers, say, "By this flame, I honour the day I came through the veil. With this light, I call upon my birth's guardian force, my protector, my guide. Wrap me in your strength and guard me on this sacred day. As I was born, so shall I be reborn into protection and power."

Take the hematite, obsidian, and amethyst in your hands, feeling their grounding and protective energy flow through you. Speak aloud your intention to shield yourself from all harm, "By stone and earth, I am grounded. By crystal and power, I am protected. No harm shall touch me; no ill shall enter. My shields are strong, my spirit whole. I walk this earth untouchable and bold."

Now sprinkle rosemary, common sage, and mugwort into the water bowl, stirring gently with your finger. As the herbs mix with the water, their cleansing energy rises. Dip your fingers in the water and anoint your forehead, heart, and feet, saying, "By herb and water, I cleanse away all that does not serve. My path and spirit are clear, and I am shielded in this sacred light." Envision any lingering negativity or dark energy dissolving into the water.

Now write down your intention for this new year of life on a small piece of paper. What do you seek to manifest? How do you wish to be protected? Fold the paper and place it on the altar under the mirror and say, "I set my intention by word and will. The universe hears me, and the cosmos align. As I walk my path, I do so in strength, power, and divine protection."

Next, hold the small mirror before your face, gazing deeply into your reflection. As you stare into your own eyes, envision a bright light surrounding you, impenetrable and glowing. This light is your shield, reflecting your true strength and magick. Now say, "I see myself clearly, empowered and whole. The light of protection shines through me. No shadow shall touch me; no ill shall pass. By my power and by the stars, I am forever guarded."

Sit in stillness for a moment, feeling the power you've raised settle into your body. Let the energy of your birthday surround you like a comforting embrace. When ready, close the circle, thanking the spirits, ancestors, and planetary forces for their protection. Do not disturb your altar until the candle has completely burned down. Do not leave the candle unattended. Snuff it out and relight it if you must leave.

5
ARCANE ALLIES

In the world of magick, wise folk are never alone. We are constantly surrounded by unseen forces that offer their protection, guidance, and power. From spirit guides to thoughtforms, these ancient beings watch over our sacred work, ensuring we are shielded from harm.

Building these connections is vital; they empower our magick and protect our sacred spaces. Servitors, for example, are advanced thoughtforms crafted for long-term tasks, serving as protectors in our rituals or guardians of our homes. Beyond these, some gatekeepers watch over the thresholds between worlds, ensuring no unwanted energies intrude on our workings. The ancient gods and goddesses of protection further fortify our craft.

The following magickal constructs and entities offer unique forms of protection and guidance. By personalising your work with them—through rituals, offerings, or the creation of servitors and thoughtforms—you deepen your connection to the unseen forces that protect and empower you. Trust in your intuition as you work with these energies, for they are not just tools, but living extensions of your magickal will.

THE GATEKEEPERS AND GUARDIANS

In the sacred practice of witchcraft, calling upon these allies is crucial for protecting your rituals, spellwork, and magickal journeys. These powerful beings stand as sentinels, guarding the thresholds between the physical and spiritual realms, ensuring that only benevolent forces enter your sacred space. Guardians can be spirits, deities, ancestors, or even elemental beings. Connecting with them creates a shield of protection that keeps negative or disruptive energies at bay. The following ritual helps you connect with and summon guardians and gatekeepers into your practice, infusing your craft with their protective presence.

ANCESTORS

Calling upon your ancestors is one of the most potent forms of protection in the practice of witchcraft. These spirits are vested in your well-being as their blood runs through your veins. Establishing a connection with your ancestors through rituals and offerings creates a protective bond that shields you from harm.

To honour your ancestors, create a dedicated altar space featuring photos, heirlooms, or items that represent your lineage. Light candles and offer food, flowers, or incense, inviting your ancestors to draw near. Say something like, "Ancestors of my blood, I call to thee, stand with me in strength, protect and guide me." Regularly tending to this altar and making offerings strengthens the bond with your ancestors, ensuring their continued protection and guidance in your life.

ANCESTRAL GUIDES

Ancestral guides, which are protective animals or spirits passed down through a family's lineage, offer unique forms of protection.

Each ancestral guide is deeply connected to a witch's heritage and can provide spiritual defence, guidance, and wisdom. Guides can be honoured through offerings or daily prayers as a shield for the witch and their loved ones. Witches can invoke their ancestral guides in rituals for protection, particularly in matters of the home, family, and personal safety by simply saying, "Spirit of my kin, through blood you flow; guard and protect wherever I go. Ancestors, guides, steer me true; with your power, I am renewed."

ANGELS AND DEVAS

Magnificent and powerful god-like supernatural beings exist across belief systems and transcend time. Two of the best-known are angels and devas. Angels, particularly archangels (the highest-ranking angels) like Michael and Raphael, act as powerful defenders against dark forces. Devas, the equivalent in Buddhism, can be called upon for protection, healing, and guidance, banishing harmful entities or energies. You can connect to them through meditation, prayer, or by using stones like selenite and clear quartz.

ASTRAL FAMILIARS

Astral familiars are spiritual beings that exist in the astral realm and serve as protectors during astral travel or dreamwork. They guide and guard witches and other wise folk when they enter the astral plane, ensuring their safety from malevolent entities and utilising astral familiars. Astral familiars are often connected to a witch's dreamwork or astral projection practices. They can be invoked before sleep to protect dreams or meditative journeys by saying, "Familiar with the stars, hear my plea, guard my spirit, wild and free. In dreams and the astral, I tread; keep me safe, by you I'm led."

CELESTIAL BEINGS

While angels are often considered celestial beings, other celestial entities can also be invoked for protection, particularly those associated with the sun, moon, and stars. Typically associated with cosmic forces, these beings can protect against spiritual and energetic threats linked to celestial cycles, such as eclipses or astrological events.

CELESTIAL SPIRITS

Protection is also offered to us from the cosmos in the form of the sun, moon, and star spirits, guarding us against psychic, energetic attacks during high solar activity. During dreamwork, astral projection, or magickal workings tied to lunar phases, one can protect against unseen forces and get guidance through challenging cosmic shifts. Invoke this assistance by saying, "Guardians of the sun, moon, and stars so bright, protect me through both day and night. By your cosmic force and light, shield my soul from sight."

DAEMONS

In ancient magickal traditions, daemons are not seen as malevolent spirits but as guiding entities that act as intermediaries between witches and the divine. These spirits are potent protectors, offering wisdom, insight, and defence against harmful energies. Daemons can serve as long-term guides in your practice, helping you navigate difficult situations. When working with daemons, it's essential to approach them with respect and reverence. Begin by researching the specific daemon you wish to work with and understanding its role and attributes.

Then, create a ritual to invoke the daemon's presence, offering gifts such as incense, wine, mead, or herbs that resonate with its energy. For example, a daemon associated with protection might be invoked to guard your home or sacred space. During the ritual, light a candle, offer incense, and speak the words of summoning: "I call upon [daemon's name], protector and guide, shield me with your ancient might." With wisdom and power, guard this place; let no harm come to those who dwell within this space."

DRAGONS

Dragons are powerful mythical beings in many magickal traditions. They are often invoked for protection, strength, and wisdom. They are ancient protectors, especially useful in defensive magick. Dragon spirits are considered highly protective of those who treat them with respect and reverence. Dragons can be invoked in protective spells to guard your sacred space, provide spiritual defence, and strengthen your aura by saying, "Ancient dragons of fire and air, shield my path with strength and care. By your flame and a mighty roar, protect my spirit forevermore."

EGREGORES

Egregores are entities formed by a group's collective thoughts and energies. Unlike servitors, egregores are not created by a single witch but by the shared intention of many. These entities grow stronger as the group's collective energy increases, and they serve as powerful protectors or guides for their group. To work with an egregore, it's essential to identify the group's shared purpose. Whether it's a coven, a family, or a close-knit community, the collective intention shapes the egregore's form and power.

Gather your group and focus on the protection or guidance you seek. As each member visualises the egregore, you can chant or perform a ritual together, infusing it with shared energy. For example, if your group is focused on protection, you might create an egregore to guard your sacred space. Visualise this being as a towering figure of light or shadow standing at the entrance to your circle, warding off negative energies. The more energy each person channels into the egregore, the stronger it becomes. To maintain the egregore's strength, it's important to continue feeding it energy through regular rituals or offerings. A group chant, lighting a candle, or even placing an object on a shared altar can renew its power. If the group's intention remains aligned with its purpose, the egregore serves as a living protector.

FETCH SPIRITS

Fetch spirits are personal spirits closely connected to the witch. They accompany witches during astral travel or magickal workings, offering protection and guidance through the unseen realms. Fetch spirits are often called upon during astral travel or journeying. Before setting out, call upon your fetch spirit to accompany and protect you. Say, "Fetch spirit, protector and guide, walk with me through the unseen. Keep me safe as I travel."

You can meet your fetch spirit through deep meditation. Visualise walking into a sacred forest or crossing into another realm where your fetch spirit awaits. Please pay attention to the forms they take, which are often animal, mythic, or even humanlike entities. They appreciate small offerings, such as honey, milk, or moon water, especially before or after rituals. You can also develop a symbol that represents your fetch spirit.

Draw it on your altar or your skin during rituals to reinforce its presence. I use my fetch spirit when drum journeying or during soul retrieval.

GODS AND GODDESSES

We focus on the gods and goddesses most invoked for ritual protection. These deities offer their energy to shield us from harm, safeguard our homes, and defend our spirits in times of need. Their presence is woven into the fabric of witchcraft, empowering our spells and enhancing our defences.

Each deity has unique powers and strengths, supporting their followers as they face life's various challenges. Following is a brief overview of these powerful deities, focusing on their role in protection rituals.

- *Anubis*—The Egyptian god of the dead, protects against negative spiritual entities and spirits. Witches call on him for spiritual cleansing and protection from harmful forces.
- *Apollo*—The Greek god of light and healing, Apollo provides clarity and protection from illness and negative spiritual influences. His light dispels darkness and maintains a balanced, pure energy.
- *Artemis*—Artemis is invoked as the Greek goddess of the hunt for personal safety and boundary protection, particularly against psychic attacks and harmful intentions.
- *Athena*—The Greek goddess of wisdom and war protects strategy and intellect. Her shield, the Aegis, is often invoked to defend psychic or spiritual battles.

- *Bast*—The Egyptian goddess of home and fertility protects households and sacred spaces. She is particularly protective of children and shields the house from negative energies.
- *Brigid*—As the Celtic goddess of the hearth, Brigid protects homes and families, offering blessings of safety and peace through her sacred flame. Her presence is often invoked in home protection rituals.
- *Freya*—The Norse goddess of love and war, Freya's protection is incredibly potent in matters of the heart. She defends witches from emotional harm and strengthens love spells with protective energy.
- *Hecate*—The goddess of witchcraft and the crossroads, Hecate, protects banishing rituals. She guides witches through the darkest times and shields them from evil forces.
- *The Morrigan*—A Celtic goddess of war and fate, the Morrigan is a fierce protector during conflict and spiritual attacks. She helps witches overcome adversity and shields them against dark forces.
- *Odin*—The All-Father in Norse mythology offers protection during spiritual warfare and divination. His wisdom and connection to the runes make him a powerful guide in magickal work.
- *Sekhmet*—In Egyptian mythology, the lioness-headed goddess of war, Sekhmet, fiercely protects against enemies and spiritual attacks. Witches call on her power to aid in banishing rituals and to protect themselves from harmful energies.
- *Thor*—The Norse god of thunder wields his hammer to break through obstacles and protect against chaos

and evil forces. His energy is direct and consequential in defensive rituals.

- *Thoth*—As the god of wisdom and magick, he plays a significant role in protection through his mastery of divine knowledge and rituals. He ensures cosmic balance and order (Ma'at), safeguarding the realms of gods and humans from chaos.

Ritual: Invoking Deities of Magickal Protection

These gods and goddesses are vital to magickal protection. When Hecate guides them through the dark, and Thor's mighty Mjolnir defends them, and Brigid protects their home, these deities shield witches' magickal work and daily lives. Through offerings and rituals, witches receive divine protection and empowerment. Try the following ritual to benefit from the deities' protection.

Needs

Representations of the deities you wish to work with, a candle for each, and protective symbols or offerings, such as your choice of herbs, stones, or incense. Additionally, you will need enough salt, of your choice, for casting a circle.

Directions

Begin by preparing your altar using representations of the gods and goddesses you wish to invoke. In this ritual example, you will be working with Hecate, Thor,

Bridgid, and Anubis. Light a candle for each deity and place protective symbols or offerings. Next, create a sacred space by casting a circle of protection around you using salt or visualisation to seal the space. Take a deep breath and focus on your intent.

Now invoke the deities by saying, "By Hecate's light and Thor's might, by Brigid's flame and Anubis's sight. I call upon you, gods and guides, to protect my spirit and stand by my side." Now offer your intent by placing your hands over your heart and speak your intent for protection, asking the deities for their shield and guidance. Finally, close the circle by extinguishing the candles and leaving offerings as thanks.

JINN

The jinn are powerful spirits from Middle Eastern lore. They are known for their ability to manipulate energy and influence the physical and spiritual realms. While they can offer substantial protection, they must be approached with caution and respect. They are honoured with offerings of incense, food, or water. Place these offerings in a sacred space or near your doorway to invite their protection. However, approach them with great respect and a clear intention. In protection rituals, say, "Jinn of the unseen realms, guardians of fire and air, I call upon your strength. Stand as protectors for me over the seen and unseen realms."

SERVITORS

Servitors are magickal constructs created by witches to carry out specific tasks or to serve as personal guardians. Unlike spirits or deities, servitors are created intentionally and brought to life through ritual, existing only for as long as you need them. Once their purpose is fulfilled, they can be reabsorbed into the ether. To create a servitor, begin by defining its purpose. What do you need protection from, and how can this servitor assist you? Perhaps you need protection while sleeping or a guardian to watch over your home.

The servitor's form can be anything you imagine, from a mythical creature to a shadowy guardian. Visualise this form in detail, seeing its every feature and attribute clearly in your mind. Once you have a clear image of the servitor, please bring it to life through ritual. Please light a candle, sprinkle herbs for protection, and call upon the elements or your personal energy to give it form. As you speak its purpose aloud, visualise energy flowing into the servitor, charging it with power. You might say, "By my will and the light of the flame, I summon you by name. A guardian to protect and defend, your power to serve until the end."

Once created, instruct the servitor on its task and give it a clear duration for its existence. If your servitor's task is to protect you during the night, visualise it standing watch as you sleep, absorbing any harmful energy that approaches. Once its purpose is complete, dismiss the servitor respectfully, thanking it and allowing its energy to dissipate or be reabsorbed into your personal power.

SHADOW GUARDIANS

Shadow guardians are entities that protect witches from hidden or internal threats. They are often invoked to guard against unconscious fears, suppressed emotions, or shadowy aspects of the self that can cause internal conflict or psychic attack. These guardians can also protect during times of profound transformation or shadow work. Call upon these entities when facing inner demons or working through profound emotional or spiritual challenges by saying, "Guardians of shadow, wise and profound, protect my soul in my darkest sleep. Through the night and inner storm, guide me back to light reborn."

THOUGHTFORMS

Thoughtforms are like servitors but are more temporary. They are created quickly through concentrated thought and intention. They are excellent for short-term tasks, such as warding off negativity during a single event or providing protection during a journey. Thoughtforms are perfect for immediate situations where you need a quick boost of protection.

To create a thoughtform, visualise a protective figure that will carry out your intention. This could be as simple as a sphere of light surrounding you or a shadowy figure that follows you as a guardian. Concentrate on this form, holding the image in your mind with clarity, and now say, "From my thoughts, I call you near, form of light, a shield to clear. For this task, your power is strong, then you return where you belong." Once the task is complete, allow the thoughtform to dissolve, thanking it for its service and visualising it as it fades into the ether.

THE WATCHERS

Watcher spirits are sometimes associated with the Grigori or fallen angels, but they are also known in some traditions as protective beings. They are often invoked to stand sentinel during rituals or periods of vulnerability. The watchers are said to be the great keepers of sacred knowledge, the first to unveil the mysteries of witchcraft, enchantment, and protection. They did not create magick, for magick has always been woven into the very fabric of existence, but they were the first to reveal its power to witches, wise folk, and seers.

Among the many, two watchers stand out for me: Azazel and Shemhazai. These beings walked the threshold between the worlds and gifted humanity the tools to protect themselves from the forces of darkness. They bestowed upon witches the power to shield, ward, and defend against the shadowed forces that sought to consume and control.

Where Azazel's magick was about creating shields, Shemhazai's gifts were more intricate, focusing on binding and warding. He taught witches how to weave magick into everyday objects, amulets, talismans, and charms, imbuing them with protective energy that could guard both the bearer and their space from harm. Shemhazai whispered the first incantations that allowed witches to call upon unseen forces to guard their homes, sacred spaces, and bodies from spiritual attack.

The spells, rituals, and enchantments we use today echo the ancient gifts given to us by Azazel and Shemhazai. They remain with us, their power rippling through time, guiding us as we continue to weave the magick of protection. Whether it's a simple ward drawn at the threshold of a door, a charm carried for protection, or a powerful spell cast under the moon's light, these acts of magickal defence are threads in a tapestry that the watchers began.

And now, in this modern age, these energies are more crucial than ever. Though we may no longer feel the watchers' presence, their gifts remain, and they are waiting for us to reclaim them. Today, we must remember the power passed down to us, the protection we can invoke, and the strength we carry as witches to stand against the forces that seek to unbalance our spirits and lives.

The watchers may no longer walk among us, but their magick flows through every spell of protection cast, every ward erected, and every boundary sealed. As you move through these pages, you will learn how to call upon this ancient wisdom to protect yourself, your loved ones, and your sacred spaces from the shadows that still linger. Remember, the power of protection magick is yours, a gift carried through time by witches like you. It is your time to weave it into your life, stand shielded by the watchers' ancient forces, and reclaim your strength in a world where the light and dark still battle for dominion.

You can use a simple invocation that opens the gateway for the watchers to enter your space. You can also carve protective symbols, such as the pentacle or the Eye of Providence, into candles or draw them on your doorways. These symbols serve as gateways for the watchers to step through. The watchers are often associated with stones such as amethyst or hematite. Keep these stones on your altar when calling upon their protection.

Create a quiet, sacred space to honour the watchers. Burn incense such as sandalwood or frankincense, which are traditionally associated with angelic beings. Then say, "Grigori, ancient watchers of the veil, I call upon you for your wisdom and protection. Guard me from harm; shield me from the unseen."

LESSER-KNOWN ENTITIES

Finally, we explore two key concepts in witchcraft: chronic spirits and gestalts, both linked to negative energy and collective thoughtforms. Chronic spirits arise from accumulated negative energy, unresolved emotions, or spiritual disturbances tied to trauma, pain, or prolonged suffering. They linger in locations, objects, or people, feeding on stagnant energy. Often connected to ancestral spirits or disturbed land spirits, they reflect energetic imprints from past events or unresolved shadow aspects of individuals.

Gestalts, on the other hand, form from collective energy. Rooted in magickal traditions, they emerge when the combined will of multiple practitioners creates a singular, powerful entity through group rituals or shared intent. Gestalts can be intentionally summoned in covens or ceremonial magick, or they may form spontaneously through shared emotions and experiences. Unlike egregores, which are consciously crafted, gestalts can arise naturally from collective consciousness.

In summary, chronic spirits manifest from unresolved energy tied to human emotions or events, while gestalts are born from collective spiritual or magickal energy, often emerging through shared rituals or experiences.

EMBRACING THE POWER OF ARCANE ALLIES

These mystical beings, whether archons guarding the higher realms, elementals embodying the forces of nature, daemons whispering ancient wisdom, or fae dancing at the edges of the wild, have woven themselves into our spiritual journey. They are the guardians and guides, the protectors and teachers who walk with us, shaping the path beneath our feet and illuminating the way forward.

Our relationships with these entities are profound and transformative in the practice of magick. Each ally brings its strengths, whether it's the grounding stability of the earth elementals, the fierce protection of the daemons, or the nurturing guidance of the ancestors. By understanding their nature and approaching them with respect and intention, we draw upon their power to enhance our work, shield us from harm, and lead us through the mysteries of the unseen world.

Our journey with these arcane allies involves deep connection and mutual respect. It is a sacred partnership that requires us to approach each interaction with a clear purpose, honouring the presence of these beings and maintaining regular communication to strengthen our bond. The more we engage with them, the more they reveal their wisdom, guiding us through the challenges and triumphs of our magickal practice.

Ritual: Connecting to the Guardians and Gatekeepers

By connecting with guardians and gatekeepers, you strengthen your rituals and magickal work with the forces of protection and guidance. These beings act as powerful allies, ensuring that no harm comes to you as you navigate the spiritual realms and work your magick. Through this sacred relationship, your practice becomes more focused, protected, and aligned with the ancient forces that have long guarded witches.

Before beginning, choose a deity or spirit who serves as a gatekeeper in your tradition. For example, Hecate is often referred to as a gatekeeper in magick, as she stands at the crossroads between worlds. Hermes (in the Greek tradition) or Anubis (in Egyptian magick) also serve as powerful gatekeepers, guiding souls and travellers through the realms.

Needs

Energy-purifying material such as smoke cleansing herb bundles (e.g., common sage), resin incense, or blessed water.

Directions

Begin by preparing your space and yourself. Cleanse your ritual area using smoke, incense, or a sprinkle of blessed water. As you do this, set your intention. Remember, you are preparing a space where only positive and protective forces may enter.

Next, say aloud, "As I cleanse this space, may only light and protection remain. All negativity and harm is banished; only the guardians of light are welcome here."

This initial cleansing ensures your space is free from unwanted energies, creating a blank slate for the guardians and gatekeepers to enter.

Now call upon the elemental guardians of the four cardinal directions: earth (north), air (east), fire (south), and water (west). Once your space is cleansed and you've chosen your guardians, begin by calling them to each of the cardinal points. You may do this by standing in the centre of your space and facing each direction, lighting a candle, or placing a symbol of each element at the appropriate point.

Turn east, speak your invocation: "Guardian of the east, protector of air, I call upon you to guard this space. Let your winds of clarity and wisdom blow through. Shield me from all harm and confusion. Now, move clockwise to face south and say, "Guardian of the south, protector of fire, I call upon you to stand as my shield;

let your flames of protection burn brightly, and guard this circle with your eternal light."

Face west, "Guardian of the west, protector of water, I call upon you to flow through this space, let your waters cleanse and shield me, guard my emotions and spirit from harm." Finally, face the north, "Guardian of the north, protector of earth, I call upon you to ground and shield this circle. Let your strength anchor this space, and guard me with your unshakable power."

As you invoke each guardian, feel their protective energy surrounding you, forming a shield around your sacred space. You may feel the air shift, the energy grows heavier or lighter, or a sense of calm and safety envelops you. Once your guardians are in place, call upon the gatekeeper to stand at the threshold of your ritual or spiritual journey. Remember, the gatekeeper's role is to protect the portal between worlds, ensuring that only the energies or spirits you invite may pass through.

To summon the gatekeeper, stand at the entrance to your ritual space or at the point where you will open a spiritual portal. Light a candle or hold a key to symbolise the gatekeeper's power.

Now speak your invocation, "Keeper of the gates, guardian of the threshold, I call upon you to stand at this portal, letting only those who come with light and good intent pass through. Protect me as I walk between worlds, shield this space from harm and deception." Feel the presence of the gatekeeper standing watch over the threshold. They now guard the space, ensuring your journey or ritual remains safe and undisturbed by negative entities or energies.

Once you have invoked your guardians and gatekeeper, spend a moment communing with them. You may ask them to reveal their presence through a sensation, image, or feeling. Please pay attention to any signs that they are near, such as a change in temperature, a sense of calm, or even visual symbols that appear in your mind.

To connect deeper, offer tokens of appreciation, such as incense, a small dish of water or salt, or herbs. Speak to them as you would a trusted ally, asking for their continued protection and guidance, by saying, "I thank you for your presence, stand strong at my side and the gates. Guide and protect me through this work, and when I am done, I release you with gratitude."

Now that your guardians and gatekeeper are in place, proceed with your ritual or magickal work, knowing that your space is shielded. Whether you're casting a protection spell, journeying between worlds, or performing divination, the presence of these powerful beings will ensure that your work is safe and protected. If, during your ritual, you feel any negative energy trying to break through, you can call upon your guardians to strengthen the shield around you.

Visualise them standing taller, their protective energy growing brighter and stronger, deflecting any harm that comes near. And now that your ritual is complete, it's important to thank and release the guardians and gatekeeper. This shows respect and ensures they are not unnecessarily bound to your space after completing their task.

Starting in the north, move counterclockwise to release each guardian. Now say, "Guardian of the north, thank you for your grounding presence. Your work here is complete; I release you with gratitude." Move to the west. "Guardian of the west, thank you for your protection and flow. I release you with thanks and honour." Move to the south, "Guardian of the south, thank you for your fiery protection. I release you with deep gratitude."

Finally, return to the east and say, "Guardian of the east, thank you for your wisdom and clarity. I release you with honour and thanks." When releasing the gatekeeper, say, "Gatekeeper of the threshold, your watch is done. Thank you for standing guard and for keeping me safe. I release you now with honour and gratitude." Visualise the energies of the guardians and gatekeeper slowly fading, leaving your space cleansed and protected in their absence.

INFUSING ENTITIES INTO YOUR WORK

Your power grows when you personalise your tools and spells and work with magickal constructs and entities designed to protect, guide, and amplify your intentions. These constructs, such as servitors, thoughtforms, elementals, and ancestral spirits, allow you to connect with forces beyond yourself, adding depth and strength to your magick.

Each entity is an ally in your practice, helping you craft robust protections and manifest your desires. By infusing your unique energy and intention into these constructs, you align with the ancient forces of the universe, making your magick personal and profoundly connected to the larger web of existence. Let's delve into the power of these entities and how to work with them to make your craft even more magickal.

The path of the witch is not one walked alone. As we align ourselves with these powerful allies, we open the door to a richer, more profound experience of magick. In their presence, the boundaries between the physical and spiritual realms begin to dissolve, and we find ourselves moving through a world where every stone, tree, and breeze holds a whisper of the divine.

These allies are more than just forces to be called upon in times of need; they are companions on our journey, each a thread in the intricate tapestry of our magickal life. As we work with them, we weave a web of protection, wisdom, and power that surrounds us, ensuring we walk our path with confidence and grace.

And so, as I close this chapter, we do so with a sense of deep gratitude and reverence for the beings who have shared their gifts with us. We leave this space not with an ending, but with a new beginning—a stronger connection to the arcane allies who will continue to guide, protect, and empower us on our journey through the mysteries of magick. With their presence, we walk hand in hand with the guardians, guides, and forces that shape the universe, forever entwined with the magick that flows through all things.

6
NATURE AND ITS SPIRITS

Nature can be a great ally in your protection work, from the flora and fauna to the spirits that reside in the earth. Plant energy, inside or outside of the home, creates natural wards against negativity. Many flowers are traditionally used in magickal workings for banishment, protection, and warding off negative forces.

Often referred to under the umbrella of fairies, nature's spirits are a diverse and widespread group of supernatural beings intricately tied to the natural world, playing specific roles in safeguarding both spaces and places. The most known and written about are the fae, of European origin. We will dive deeper into how these sacred energies can help you with protection magick.

GUARDIANS OF THORN AND BRANCH

I was connected to the land and its sacred energies from a young age. One of my earliest and most vivid memories is travelling to Caithness, to Auntie Barbara's farm. The land was wild and untamed, and her home stood proudly, surrounded by a full circle with a driveway into the farm of blackthorn (*Prunus spinosa*) and hawthorn (*Crataegus monogyna*) as if the very earth had wrapped her in a protective embrace.

It was within this natural barrier that I first learned the magickal properties of these ancient trees. Auntie Barbara spoke of them as hedging trees and guardians of the land, each carrying a power that has stayed with me ever since. Blackthorn, with its dark, twisted branches, symbolised protection through strength and resilience, fending off all who might bring harm. Hawthorn was a tree of healing and heart, a force of love and protection that invited peace while warding away negativity.

Even then, I knew that I was learning something ancient, something that would shape the way I viewed magick forever.

The lessons I learned around those trees have never left me. They became the foundation for how I approach the tools and elements of my practice, recognising that nature's gifts are not mere ingredients but living allies in the craft.

BLACKTHORN

Known as the Witch's Tree, blackthorn is a powerful symbol of protection and defence. With its dark thorny branches, blackthorn creates a natural boundary, both physically and energetically, warding off harmful influences. In magick, blackthorn is often used in banishing spells to repel negativity and break curses. Carrying a staff or wand made from blackthorn can serve as a potent shield against psychic attacks, while placing its thorns around your home can keep evil forces at bay. Its energy is fierce, making it a powerful ally when you need strength and resilience in your protective workings.

HAWTHORN

Hawthorn, known as the Faerie Tree, carries a softer yet equally potent form of protection. Traditionally planted as hedges around homes, hawthorn is believed to guard against evil spirits and misfortune. It invites peace and love while keeping harm and negative energies away. Magickly, hawthorn is used to protect the heart, both emotionally and spiritually, making it a perfect ally for spells focused on harmony and healing. Hanging its blossoms in your home or creating a protective talisman from its wood helps create a peaceful boundary, safeguarding your space with gentle strength.

OTHER TREES OF NOTE

- *Ash* (*Fraxinus excelsior*)—Defending against negative forces, creating powerful protective staffs and wands, guarding against illness and harmful entities, protection during travel or transitions, balancing and grounding protective energies.
- *Birch* (*Betula pendula*)—Cleansing and protection from negative energy, warding off harmful spirits.
- *Elder* (*Sambucus nigra*)—Protecting against evil spirits and curses, providing spiritual protection during rituals, banishing unwanted energies, creating powerful protective amulets, and connecting to ancestral spirits for guidance.
- *Hazel* (*Corylus avellana*)—Protecting against negativity and psychic attack, empowering magickal tools and charms, guarding sacred knowledge and wisdom, strengthening divination and intuition for protection.
- *Holly* (*Ilex aquifolium*)—Protection from malevolent spirits and enchantments, deflecting psychic attacks and curses,

strengthening courage and resilience in protection spells, guarding against bad luck and misfortune.

- ***Oak*** (*Quercus robur*)—Strength and stability in protective workings, guarding homes and sacred spaces, empowering spells with courage and resilience, warding off negativity and harmful energies, protection during times of change or conflict.
- ***Pine*** (*Pinus sylvestris*)—Cleansing and clearing negative energy, protecting sacred spaces and the home, shielding against harmful influences, empowering protection during purification, protecting new beginnings and transitions, banishing evil or unwanted influences.
- ***Rowan*** (*Sorbus aucuparia*)—Protection from enchantment and dark magick, warding off malevolent spirits, empowering charms and amulets, safeguarding travellers and strengthening psychic shields.
- ***Willow*** (*Salix alba*)—Protection during emotional healing, warding off negative energy in sacred spaces, safeguarding against psychic attacks and emotional harm, creating protective tools for intuitive work and dream protection.
- ***Yew*** (*Taxus baccata*)—Protection from death-related energies, shielding from hexes and curses, guarding sacred burial sites or ancestral lands, creating powerful tools for spirit work and protection, connecting to ancient wisdom and protective spirits.

FABULOUS FLORA

Flora in all its forms has always been an ally in protection. Flowers, for example, are frequently associated with beauty and softness, yet they carry potent protective energies. Many flowers are traditionally used in magickal workings for banishment, protection, and warding off negative forces.

Yet, in many modern homes, plants are often absent, leaving spaces devoid of this vital protective force. Indoor plants enhance the environment with their beauty and strengthen the energy, creating a natural barrier against harm and unwanted influences. Their ability to cleanse, shield, and protect is unmatched, making them essential companions in magickal workings and daily life.

Here is a list of the most common houseplants and their attributes for magickal protection:

- *Aloe Vera* (*Aloe barbadensis miller*)—Great for absorbing negative energy, protecting against accidents and misfortune, and promoting healing and peace.
- *Basil* (*Ocimum basilicum*)—Wards off negative spirits, promotes protection and peace, used in protective charms or near doorways to guard against harm.
- *Bay Laurel* (*Laurus nobilis*)—Protects against negative energy and evil influences, promotes strength, and wards off harm when placed near doorways and windows.
- *Chrysanthemum* (*Chrysanthemum morifolium*)—Protects against evil spirits and negative energy. Used in protection spells for the home and family. Enhances stability and peace in times of stress.
- *Dandelion* (*Taraxacum officinale*)—Represents strength and the ability to overcome obstacles. Used in banishment rituals and protective charms. Protects against unwanted spirits and emotional harm.
- *Heather* (*Calluna vulgaris*)—The flowers are associated with peace, protection, and spiritual

guardianship. Used in spells to protect against unwanted spirits and harm. Placed in sachets or around the home for protection and tranquillity.

- ***Honeysuckle*** (*Lonicera japonica*)—Attracts positive energy while repelling hostile forces. Used in protection spells to shield against harmful intentions. Vital for guarding the home and creating a safe space.
- ***Ivy*** (*Hedera helix*)—Guards against unwanted energies, protects the home's boundaries, and brings a sense of security and protection.
- ***Jasmine*** (*Jasminum officinale*)—Protects against negative spirits; encourages love, peace, and harmony; and attracts positive energy while dispelling negativity.
- ***Lavender*** (*Lavandula angustifolia*)—Protects against negative energy and emotional harm. Used in spells for peace, protection, and purification. Vital for psychic protection and guarding the home.
- ***Marigold*** (*Tagetes erecta*)—Known for its protective properties against spiritual attack. Used to banish harmful influences and create protective boundaries. Strong for shielding the home from curses and negativity.
- ***Mint*** (*Mentha* spp.)—Wards off negative spirits and harmful energies and promotes protection and peace, encouraging revitalising energy for the home.
- ***Peace Lily*** (*Spathiphyllum wallisii*)—Purifies the air and energy in the home, protecting against negativity and promoting harmony to restore peace and balance to the household.
- ***Rosemary*** (*Salvia rosmarinus*)—Wards off harmful spirits and energy, enhances protection and

purification, and promotes clarity and peaceful energy in the home.

- *Rose* (*Rosa × damascena*)—Wards off negative energies while promoting love and peace. Used in protection spells, especially around relationships. Creates a protective shield around the heart.
- *Rowanberries* (*Fructus sorbi*)—Ward off evil. Used in charms and amulets to safeguard against negative influences and often carried or placed near windows and doorways for personal and home protection.
- *Snake Plant* (*Dracaena trifasciata*)—Cleanses negative energy from the environment, acts as a shield for the home, grounds and stabilises the energy in the space.
- *Spider Plant* (*Chlorophytum comosum*)—Cleanses and purifies the air and energy, protects against negative influences, and shields the home from external stress.
- *Sunflowers* (*Helianthus annuus*)—Associated with protection and positivity. Used to ward off harmful spirits and invite happiness into the home. Strong for personal protection and creating a protective aura.
- *Thistle* (*Cirsium vulgare*)—Symbol of resilience and strong protection. Used to ward off unwanted spirits and negative energy. Placed around the home or carried for defence against harm.
- *Vervain* (*Verbena officinalis*)—Traditionally used in protective charms and amulets. Wards off evil spirits and negative energies. Great for personal protection and cleansing.

- *Yarrow* (*Achillea millefolium*)—Strengthens psychic protection and shields against negativity. Used in spells to create protective boundaries around the home. Enhances courage and resilience in protection rituals.

NATURE'S SPIRITS

These magickal beings are interwoven throughout the natural world and the various elemental forces at play. Always approach the fae with respect. It is then that they can offer protection, healing, and insight.

Most other types of spirits, including brownies, pixies, dryads, sylphs, salamanders, gnomes, undines, and kelpies, serve as guardians of specific sacred natural places such as forests, rivers, mountains, and groves. Some can be particularly helpful in safeguarding your home or sacred space.

ELEMENTALS

Elementals are ancient spirits that embody the four fundamental forces of nature: earth, air, fire, and water. Wise folk, witches, and Indigenous peoples around the world have called upon these spirits for centuries, and they offer unique protective energies depending on the elements they represent.

Their names and descriptions may vary slightly, depending on where in the world you are, but they are duty bound to the air, fire, water, and earth, which they are born to protect and manipulate, as follows:

- *Earth elementals* offer grounding and stability. The most known are dwarves, gnomes, and leprechauns. These entities are deeply connected to the land, providing solid and unwavering strength and protection. To work with earth elementals, place stones or crystals on your altar and call upon them to ground you in stability and protection.

- *Air elementals*, which include sylphs, zephyrs, griffins, and harpies, bring clarity and swiftness to your protection, sweeping away negative energies with the force of the wind. You can work with air elements by hanging feathers or burning incense to carry your prayers and intentions skyward.
- *Fire elementals* offer transformation and fierce protection, burning away harmful energies that seek to harm you. Lighting a candle or bonfire and calling on the flame's spirit can summon fire elementals to stand as guardians.
- *Water elementals* provide emotional protection and purification, cleansing away psychic residue and harmful influences. To work with water elementals, use blessed water, stormwater, or moon water in your rituals, calling on their fluid, calming energy to protect and purify your space.

CONNECT WITH THE FAE

The fae are deeply tied to natural places. Connect with them by spending time in nature, particularly in areas such as forests, groves, or rivers. Leave small offerings, such as honey, milk, or shiny objects (like coins or crystals) in places where you sense their presence. Dedicate a small section of your garden or home to the fae. Plant flowers, leave tiny offerings, and invite the fae to visit. Be sure to keep the space clean and tended, as the fae appreciate beauty and order. And if you are working in a natural setting, call upon the fae to guard your circle and lend their protection. To do this, you can say, "Fae of the forest, land, and sky, I call upon you with offerings in hand. Bless this circle with your protection and wisdom."

CONNECT WITH OTHER NATURE SPIRITS

Nature spirits appreciate offerings like fresh flowers, water, stones, or food left at the base of trees, by streams, or in other natural settings. Acknowledge their presence by speaking words of gratitude for the protection they provide. Spend time outdoors, attuning yourself to the energies around you. Feel the wind, the earth beneath your feet, and the water's flow. Listen to the subtle whispers of the spirits within the trees and stones. This practice will deepen your connection with the guardians of the land.

Create an altar or sacred space in your home honouring the nature spirits. Use symbols like leaves, stones, or feathers to represent the elements of the natural world. When seeking protection, say, "Spirits of the land, protectors of the earth, I honour your presence and call upon your strength. Guard this space, my home, and my heart."

7
TALISMANS AND SACRED SUPPLIES

Your surroundings offer a wealth of powerful items that can be woven into spells, charms, and rituals. Crystals, stones, feathers, seashells, and other natural objects are gifts from the earth, sky, and sea, each carrying unique energy. These objects have deep connections to the elements and serve as potent tools for protection, grounding, and empowerment. Whether gathered from the land or the ocean, these sacred talismans can enhance magickal workings, strengthen protective barriers, and serve as personal amulets to ward off negativity.

MINERAL PERFECTION AND PROTECTION

Crystals hold the ancient energies of the earth, making them powerful tools for protection, banishment, and binding in magickal work. Each crystal resonates with a unique frequency that can shield against negativity, absorb harmful energies, or reflect malicious intent.

Incorporating crystals into your spells and rituals creates substantial, energetic barriers that guard your physical, emotional, and spiritual self. Whether worn as amulets, placed in protective grids, or carried for personal shielding, crystals provide a solid foundation for powerful magickal protection.

- *Amethyst*—Protects against spiritual harm and psychic attack, enhances psychic defence and intuition, and wards off negative energies during sleep and dreamwork.
- *Apache Tear*—Protects against grief, sorrow, and negative emotions. Absorbs and transmutes harmful energy. Strong for personal healing and protection during emotional work.
- *Black Tourmaline*—Absorbs negative energy and psychic attacks, grounding and protecting the aura. Is powerful for creating protective grids in the home.
- *Bloodstone*—Grounds and protects against negative energy. Enhances courage and strength in protective rituals. Strong for shielding the aura and body in challenging situations.
- *Carnelian*—Protects against envy, resentment, and psychic attacks. It provides personal courage and strengthens the aura. Used to banish fear and protect personal boundaries.
- *Clear Quartz*—Amplifies protective energy in spells and rituals. Cleanses and shields the aura from harmful forces. Used to strengthen the energy of other protective crystals.
- *Fluorite*—Cleanses and purifies the aura. Protects against psychic attack and energy drain. Vital for mental clarity and shielding the mind.
- *Garnet*—Protects transitions and times of vulnerability. Shields the body and aura from negativity.

Used to strengthen personal boundaries and banish harmful influences.

- *Hematite*—Deflects negative energy and psychic attacks. Strengthens personal protection and grounding. Shields the mind from harmful thoughts and interference.
- *Jet*—Absorbs negativity and dispels harmful energy. Used for protection in rituals involving banishment and binding. Shields the home from dark forces.
- *Labradorite*—Shields the aura and protects against psychic attack. Reflects negative energy away from the body. Vital for spiritual protection and dreamwork.
- *Lapis Lazuli*—Guards against psychic attack and spiritual interference. Strengthens personal boundaries and intuition. Used for spiritual protection during meditation and dreamwork.
- *Malachite*—Absorbs negative energy and shields the heart. Vital for protection in emotional healing and spiritual growth. Used to guard against psychic attack and harmful intentions.
- *Obsidian*—Acts as a shield against negative energy and harmful intentions. Vital for banishing and grounding unwanted forces. Powerful for protection in personal spaces and rituals.
- *Pyrite*—Deflects negativity and shields against harm. Strengthens protective energy for financial security. Used in protective charms for abundance and prosperity.
- *Red Jasper*—Grounds and stabilises energy for personal protection. Shields against emotional harm

and energy depletion. Used in protective amulets for strength and resilience.

- *Selenite*—Clears and purifies negative energy from spaces and objects. Strengthens personal protection and raises spiritual vibration. Used in protective grids to create sacred space.
- *Shungite*—Absorbs and neutralises negative energy and electromagnetic radiation; cleanses and protects the aura and personal space. Vital for shielding from harmful environmental energies.
- *Smoky Quartz*—Transmutes negative energy into positive energy; grounds and protects against unwanted influences. Used to cleanse and protect the aura.
- *Tiger's Eye*—Wards off negative energy and malicious intent. Promotes courage and confidence in protective magick. Grounds and strengthens the personal energy field.

ELEMENTAL STONES

Stones are not just physical objects; they carry the energy of the elements from which they come. Whether formed in the depths of the sea, born from volcanic fire, or found atop mountains, each stone holds the power of its origin, making it a powerful tool in protection, healing, and transformation. By connecting to these elemental energies, we can tap into the forces of nature to protect, ground, and shield ourselves from harm.

As I sit and write, I am surrounded by stones I've gathered from all around the world, each one connected to the elements and places it comes from. These stones ground me in the earth's energy as I work, offering protection and stability. Stones can be used in medicine wheels, healing circles, and personal protection spells, allowing us to tap into their elemental power.

- *Basalt (Earth)*—Formed from volcanic rock, it holds intense grounding energy and protection. Used for anchoring energy and protecting sacred spaces. Vital for stability during times of change and transformation.
- *Desert Rose (Wind/Earth)*—Found in desert environments, it holds the energy of wind and earth combined. Used to protect against negative influences and psychic attack. Vital for shielding the mind and enhancing clarity in spiritual work.
- *Lava Stone (Fire)*—Born from volcanic eruptions, it holds the raw energy of fire. Powerful for transformation, protection, and banishing negativity. Used to ground and burn away harmful energy.
- *Mountain Stones (Air)*—Found on mountaintops, these stones connect to the element of air and spiritual clarity. Used for protection in higher spiritual work and psychic defence. Strong for grounding thoughts and bringing focus during rituals.
- *Obsidian (Fire)*—Formed from molten lava, it holds the energy of fire for banishing and protection. Used to cut away negative attachments and shield against psychic attacks. Powerful for creating protective barriers in personal and ritual spaces.
- *River Stones (Water)*—Shaped by the flow of water, they bring the energy of emotional balance and protection. Used to create calm, protective spaces in the

home. Strong for personal grounding and emotional cleansing.

- *Seabed Stones (Water)*—Formed deep in the oceans, they carry the calming and cleansing energy of water. Used to soothe emotional turmoil and protect from emotional harm. Powerful for purification and connecting to intuition.
- *Seer Stone (Water)*—Also known as window quartz or river-polished quartz, it carries the energy of water and intuition. Used for divination, scrying, and protection in psychic work. Strong for shielding the mind and connecting to hidden knowledge.
- *Slate (Earth)*—A stone of deep grounding, it absorbs and neutralises harmful energy. Used in protective circles and grids to guard against spiritual interference. Vital for shielding during emotional healing.
- *Tektite (Air/Fire)*—A stone formed from meteoric impacts, holding the energy of both air and fire. Used for spiritual protection and connection to higher realms. Strong for shielding the aura and deflecting harmful energy from external sources.

SALT OF THE EARTH

Salt, a powerful crystal and gift from the earth, has long been revered for its protective and purifying properties. In magick, salt is a barrier against hostile forces, banishing harmful spirits and cleansing spaces of stagnant energy. Salt is one of the most potent tools in a witch's arsenal, whether used in circles for protection, sprinkled around doorways, or dissolved in water for purification.

Each type of salt carries its unique energy, adding different layers of strength and defence to magickal workings.

- *Black Salt*—Also known as Kala Namak, a kiln-fired rock salt. Absorbs negative energy and breaks curses, protecting against psychic attacks and harmful forces. It is often used in banishing rituals and warding.
- *Blackthorn Salt*—Crafted from wind, sea, and thorns on the West Coast of Scotland. Is used in powerful banishing and binding spells. Wards off dark spirits and harmful influences; strengthens protective boundaries around the home.
- *Blessed Salt*—Consecrated for spiritual protection. Used in creating sacred circles and for home protection. Enhances purification in rituals.
- *Blue Salt (Persian Salt)*—Strengthens communication and protection of the spirit.
- *Epsom Salt*—Used for personal cleansing and aura protection. Removes negative energy from the body in ritual baths. Promotes relaxation and healing while strengthening protective energy.
- *Pink Himalayan Salt*—Cleanses and balances energy. Provides gentle protection for the home and personal space. Enhances spiritual and emotional protection.
- *Red Salt (Hawaiian Salt)*—Grounding and protection in banishing work. Guards against misfortune and opposing forces. Used to protect sacred spaces and connect to the earth's energy.

- *Sea Salt*—Purifies spaces and cleanses energy. Creates substantial protective barriers in rituals. Used in sacred circles for grounding and protection.
- *Smoked Salt*—Adds strength to banishing and protective spells. Used to protect the home and sacred spaces. Wards off harmful energies with added potency from fire and smoke. Used in rituals to guard against psychic interference. Protects spiritual work and dreamwork.

LIGHTNING WOOD

There is a rare and potent power in wood that has been struck by lightning. This wood holds the raw, electrifying energy of the storm, making it a highly sought-after tool for protection, binding, and banishment. Lightning wood channels the force of nature, embodying both destruction and creation. When used in magickal workings, it acts as a conduit of pure power, amplifying spells and rituals that call for solid defences or the banishment of harmful energies.

Carved into staffs, wands, staves, or stangs, lightning wood becomes a powerful weapon in the witch's arsenal. A staff made from lightning-struck wood can draw protective circles, its energy forming an unbreakable barrier. Wands and staves crafted from this sacred wood can direct energy precisely, making them ideal for binding spells or banishment rituals. The stang, a forked staff traditionally used in witchcraft, channels this energy to guard sacred spaces, ensuring no ill will crosses its threshold.

GRAVEYARD DIRT

Another powerful and often misunderstood material is graveyard dirt. Sourced respectfully from an ancestor's grave, this material carries the energy of the resting place, making it useful for protection, boundary work, and ancestral magick.

In protection work, graveyard dirt is often sprinkled around the perimeter of a home or space to create a protective barrier. It can also be used in spells to bring the protective energy of the spirits into your work, guarding against psychic attacks or malicious influences.

BONE

Working with bone can add a strong layer of protection to magick. Bones are connected to both the ancestors and the physical realm, offering protection from beyond the veil. Bone amulets or charms are often used to guard against harmful spirits, and bones placed in the corners of a home serve as silent watchers, protecting the space.

CASTING THE BONES FOR MAGICKAL PROTECTION

Casting bones, or osteomancy, is an ancient divinatory practice that witches have used to seek guidance and protection. Bones, connected to death and the ancestral realm, carry powerful energy to be tapped into for shielding and defence. When used in protective magick, the bones are cast onto a surface, and their arrangement is interpreted to reveal messages about potential threats or areas where protection is needed.

To perform this ritual, gather bones that resonate with you, whether animal or bird bones; each carries its unique energy. Hold them in your hands, setting a clear intention for protection.

As you cast the bones onto the surface, watch how they fall. The patterns they create can reveal areas of vulnerability, opportunities for increased magickal protection, or hidden dangers.

BRIMSTONE (SULPHUR)

Sulphur, or brimstone, has been historically used in protection and banishing. Its pungent smell drives away evil spirits, making it useful in protection circles or sprinkled around areas that need heavy-duty shielding. Sulphur is often combined with other protective herbs and materials in spell jars or sprinkled around homes to purify and create a strong barrier.

THE FLOW OF PROTECTION

Water is one of the most ancient and powerful elements, carrying the essence of life, transformation, and purification. In magickal protection, water becomes a conduit for cleansing negative energy, creating spiritual barriers, and blessing sacred spaces. By harnessing the natural power of water, witches tap into the cycles of the earth and sky, invoking the strength of nature to guard and protect. Each type of water, whether gathered from a storm or drawn from a mountain spring, holds unique energies that can be used to empower rituals and strengthen protective spells.

- *Holy Water*—Any form of consecrated water for ultimate spiritual protection. Wards off negative entities and energy in the home. Used to bless and purify spaces, objects, and people.
- *Moon Water*—Charged under the light of the moon. Offers spiritual and emotional protection. Used in rituals for psychic defence and dream protection.

Strengthens protective boundaries in the home and sacred spaces.

- *Mountain Water*—Water from its source, or the original first pool or stream. Holds the untouched purity and power of nature. It protects from spiritual interference and unwanted influences. Used in rituals to strengthen personal and environmental protection.
- *Ocean Water*—Represents the vast power of the sea, protecting against dark forces and harmful spirits. Used in banishing solid rituals to cleanse and purify. Shields the home from negativity and psychic attack.
- *Rainwater*—Symbolises cleansing and renewal, washing away negativity and harmful energy. It provides gentle protection and purifies spaces. Used to cleanse objects and tools of stagnant energy.
- *River Water*—Carries the energy of movement and flow, protecting against stagnation and blockages. Used to cleanse spaces of lingering harmful energy. It protects travellers and provides a sense of direction and clarity.
- *Snow Water*— From melted snow. Represents stillness and calm, freezing out negativity and spiritual threats. Used to freeze harmful energies or people from causing harm. Protects during times of emotional healing and vulnerability.
- *Spring Water*—Purifies and renews energy in the home. Provides gentle but firm protection for emotional and spiritual well-being. Used in cleansing rituals to wash away negativity.
- *Stormwater*—Collected during a storm. Charged with the power of the storm, it provides intense

protection. Used in banishing rituals to remove negativity. Strengthens spells of transformation and cleansing.

- *Well Water*—Holds ancient, profound earth energy for grounding and protection. Draws on the wisdom of ancestors and the spirit of the land. Used to protect the home and guard against negative entities.

METALS

Metals are powerful in witchcraft. They are often used to craft tools like athames, swords, and jewellery, all imbued with protective energy. Each metal has unique vibrations and properties, making it an essential element in magickal protection.

- *Bronze*, an ancient alloy of copper and tin, symbolises endurance and strength. It's frequently used in amulets, talismans, and tools like cauldrons or statues. In protection magick, bronze is believed to stabilise energy, helping the wearer or practitioner stay grounded while warding off hostile forces.
- *Copper* is a highly conductive metal, often used in magick for protection and energy flow. It enhances the power of protective spells by amplifying energy and balancing forces, making it ideal for crafting amulets, wands, and jewellery. Copper's natural properties create a shield of protection while harmonising spiritual and physical energies.
- *Silver*, often associated with the moon and feminine energy, is a metal of purification and protection. It's commonly used in jewellery and ritual tools to enhance psychic protection, reflect harmful energy,

and create a barrier against negativity. Witches often wear silver jewellery or use silver tools in their rituals to strengthen their connection to the spiritual realms while remaining shielded from harm.

THE POWER OF IRON

Iron has long been revered in witchcraft and folklore. It is known for its incredible power to ward off evil spirits and dark forces. Throughout the ages, witches have recognised iron as one of the most potent natural protectors, creating an unbreakable barrier between the physical and spiritual realms. For witches, iron's power comes from its connection to the earth's core, grounding and stabilising energy while creating an impenetrable shield. When iron is forged in fire, it absorbs the transformative power of that element, making it a formidable weapon against spiritual attacks.

In protection magick, iron can be used in various forms, whether as nails placed at the corners of a home, as iron jewellery worn for personal defence, or as an ingredient in spellwork. It is particularly effective in banishing rituals, where its energy helps break curses, dispel negative influences, and sever unwanted spiritual connections.

One of the most well-known uses of iron is the horseshoe, which is believed to protect against spirits and attract good fortune. Placed above doorways, horseshoes act as both a guardian and a talisman, ensuring the household remains safe and prosperous.

When working with iron in your witchcraft, you draw upon centuries of tradition and align yourself with one of the earth's most potent protectors. Its grounding energy will shield you and connect you deeply to the earth's ancient magick.

Coffin nails hold a unique place in protection and banishing magick. Traditionally, they are iron nails taken from old coffins, and their connection to death and the underworld makes them potent tools for banishing negativity and warding off dark spirits. When used in spells, coffin nails are often placed at the four corners of a home to create an impenetrable boundary of protection.

They can also be used in jars or buried near the threshold to block unwanted energy from entering. The energy of the nails serves as a final resting place for curses or evil forces, ensuring they are laid to rest permanently.

Rusty nails, though not as widely known as coffin nails, are often used in similar protective work. The rust symbolises decay and the destruction of opposing forces, making them ideal for banishing spells. Rusty nails can be placed in poppets, spell jars, or buried around the home to break hexes and protect against lingering negative energy.

Crafting with metals like silver, copper, bronze, or even iron allows witches to harness the natural protective properties of these materials. They ensure that the items they create, whether tools, jewellery, or other magickal objects, act as continuous shields, offering spiritual and physical defence.

FROM THE KITCHEN

The kitchen is more than a place for nourishment; it's also a sacred space where magick is brewed daily. Many common kitchen ingredients carry powerful protective properties that witches have used for centuries. These everyday foods serve as potent allies in magickal protection, whether for warding off negative energy, strengthening spells, or creating protective barriers.

By incorporating these witchy foods into your magickal practice, you can transform your kitchen into a place of power and protection.

- ***Basil*** (*Ocimum basilicum*)—Wards off harmful spirits. Protects against curses and negativity. Promotes peace and protection in the home.
- ***Bay Leaves*** (*Laurus nobilis*)—Wards off evil spirits and negative energy. Protects the home and sacred spaces. Used in protective charms and amulets.
- ***Black Pepper*** (*Piper nigrum*)—Repels unwanted spirits and energy. Used in banishing spells and protection rituals. Adds a sharp, defensive energy to protective workings.
- ***Cinnamon*** (*Cinnamomum verum*)—Protects against negative energy and harmful forces. It brings warmth and protection to the home. Used in protective charms and spells.
- ***Clove*** (*Syzygium aromaticum*)—Wards off evil spirits and negative influences. Strengthens personal protection spells. Often burned or used in protection charms.
- ***Garlic*** (*Allium sativum*)—Wards off evil spirits and harmful entities. Protects the home from negative influences. Strengthens personal protection and well-being.
- ***Honey***—Seals protective charms and spells. Draws positive energy while warding off negativity. Used to sweeten and strengthen protective workings.
- ***Onions*** (*Allium cepa*)—Absorbs and banishes negative energy. Protects against illness and

psychic attack. Traditionally hung in the home for protection.

- *Vinegar*—Cleanses and purifies spaces. Breaks curses and banishes negative energy. Strengthens protective spells and rituals.

ADDITIONAL NATURAL RESOURCES

- *Driftwood*—Symbol of resilience and protection after hardship. Used in protective talismans and charms for personal strength. Strong for grounding and shielding in protection spells.
- *Feathers*—Symbol of air and spirit, they carry messages from the divine. Used in protective charms for spiritual defence and guidance. Often placed in windows or above doorways to ward off harm.
- *Honeycomb*—Symbol of protection and unity within a community. Used in spells to create harmony and protect the home. Often placed on altars or carried to promote peace and security.
- *Oak Acorns*—Symbol of strength and protection from harm. Used in protective charms and carried for personal strength and resilience. Strong for grounding and stability in protective spells.
- *Pine Cones*—Associated with protection and purification. Placed in homes or sacred spaces to ward off negativity and promote harmony. Often used in charms for protection during seasonal transitions.
- *Seashells*—Connected to the water element and the energy of the sea. Used for protection and emotional healing.

Powerful for guarding sacred spaces and bringing peace to the home.

- *Snakeskin*—Represents transformation and protection against harm. Used in rituals for shedding negativity or spiritual rebirth. Strong for personal protection and renewal spells. Collect ethically (sheddings—do not skin).

8

THE SACRED BODY

Throughout many world religions and even older belief systems, the body has been seen as a sacred vessel, housing the spirit and connecting us to the magickal forces of the universe. For witches, the skin, for example, has often served as a canvas for protection, a means to channel energy and fortify the self against harm. This chapter examines the primary attributes and areas of the body utilised in magickal protection and their rationale.

THE SKIN

Tattoos, as with all other sacred markings etched into the skin, are more than mere decoration; they are magickal seals, protective symbols, and personal spells that resonate with the body's energy. As such, tattoos constantly charge the body with energy and protection. When we intentionally ink these marks onto our skin, we are sealing a spell into ourselves. Each mark made holds power, and these markings serve as protective barriers against the forces that seek to harm or drain us.

And because tattoos are not for everyone, drawing body sigils with oil is an effective, nonpermanent way to tap into this technique and shield yourself from negative energies, harmful intentions, or psychic attacks. This practice allows you to mark your body with sacred symbols without the permanence, or for some people, the prohibitive cost of tattoos, creating temporary magickal barriers that empower and protect.

HAIR AND NAILS

Throughout the ages, witches have recognised the power in their hair and nails; these seemingly simple extensions of the self are potent conduits for energy. To allow another to possess even a strand of your hair or a clipping of your nails is to hand over a piece of your essence, a key to your power. Hair, flowing with life force, and nails, formed of hardened protection, are bound to your energy field. As witches, we must be ever watchful of where these fragments of our bodies end up.

In the old ways, witches would burn their fallen hair and nail clippings, ensuring no one could use them for ill intent. To this day, we keep this sacred practice, never leaving behind traces of ourselves for others to collect and weave into spells. Protecting your hair and nails means guarding your energy from manipulation, ensuring your power remains yours.

For those seeking to deepen this practice, it's common to anoint the hair with protective oils or tie knots into strands, weaving spells of strength and shielding. Nails can also be anointed, drawing symbols of protection onto them or incorporating them into personal spellwork, keeping your energy fiercely guarded. As witches, safeguarding your hair and nails is a potent self-defence practice that ensures you remain sovereign over your spirit. Never forget that your power is in every part of you, and it must always be protected.

MAGICKAL MAKEUP PROTECTION

In the swirling sands of times gone by, witches, priestesses, and queens alike knew the secret art of makeup. It wasn't merely for beauty; it was a sacred form of protection, a spell painted upon the skin. The magick of makeup traces its lineage back to the lands of Egypt, where even the sun god Ra and the goddess Isis lent their divine essence to the pigments and powders used by their followers. But this ancient wisdom is not lost to us. We, too, can summon that power, channelling the magick of protection through our makeup. When you paint your eyes with precision or anoint your face with sacred oils in the early morning hours, remember that you are tapping into this long-forgotten art of protection. You cast a spell upon yourself that guards your spirit and strengthens your energy as you step into the world.

Today, you can use makeup to weave magick into your daily life. Each line of eyeliner can serve as a barrier, each shade of lipstick a sigil of power. Our makeup becomes part of our magickal armour, protecting our energy, warding off unwanted influences, and enhancing our inner strength. As you gaze into your mirror, remember: You are a modern-day magickian, invoking the ancient art of sacred protection through the magick of makeup. Let your face become the canvas upon which you draw your spells, each stroke a testament to the wisdom of those who came before us. Let your beauty be your shield, your magick, your power.

SACRED ENERGY POINTS FOR MAGICKAL PROTECTION

Beyond ink and markings, the body contains powerful energy points, places where magick flows most freely, and protection can be invoked and strengthened. The third eye, the hands, the feet, the heart, and the crown of the head are just a few of these sacred gateways, and when we consciously work with them, we unlock immense power to shield ourselves from harm.

THE THIRD EYE

Located on the forehead between the eyebrows, the third eye is the seat of psychic vision and intuition. Protecting this area shields you from psychic attacks and negative influences while also enhancing your ability to see beyond the veil.

THE CROWN

At the top of the head, the crown chakra connects us to divine energies. Protection here ensures we remain spiritually grounded, keeping harmful energies from entering this sacred gateway.

THE MEDULLA OBLONGATA

In magickal protection, we access the medulla oblongata, which is a sacred gateway where spirit enters and energy flows between worlds at the base of the neck. This place is often regarded as the passageway for spiritual forces, making it an essential point to guard for any witch or seeker who communes with unseen realms. Left unprotected, it can invite unwelcome energies, making it crucial to shield this portal carefully. With each anointing, each sigil, and each protective mark, you reclaim your power and stand as the sole gatekeeper of your sacred energy flow.

Amber oil is a perfect ally for protecting the medulla oblongata. Before you begin your magickal workings, anoint the base of your neck with amber, feeling its warm energy form a protective barrier. This golden essence binds the gateway, allowing only the highest vibrations to enter while keeping hostile forces at bay. For those who seek more permanent protection, consider a tattoo at this sacred spot, etched with magickal intent to guard the spiritual doorway forever.

THE HANDS

As power conduits, the hands craft spells, direct energy, and protect the self. Symbols of protection, such as pentacles, can be inscribed or imagined on the palms to fortify the magick that flows from your hands.

THE HEART

Protecting the heart centre is crucial for shielding emotions and ensuring no harmful energy can disrupt the flow of love, compassion, and inner strength. Symbols like the triple moon or sacred animals can guard this area, ensuring emotional resilience.

THE FEET

The feet ground us to the earth, the most ancient source of protection. Inscribing symbols of strength, such as runes for stability or sigils for grounding, ensures that we walk through life protected and centred.

CHOOSING OILS FOR BODY PROTECTION

Essential oils are potent allies in magickal and energetic protection. Each oil carries a unique vibration and spirit, and when used intentionally, they can help shield the aura, strengthen boundaries, and clear out negative energy. Used with care, they become spiritual armour, anchoring your energy, clearing your space, and weaving protection into your daily practice. The oils listed are ancient and trusted for their protective qualities.

- *Frankincense* is known for spiritual protection; this oil creates a powerful shield around your energy.
- *Rosemary* is a classic oil for protection; rosemary wards off negative energy and clears the aura.
- *Sandalwood* provides grounding and shields your energy, creating a barrier against psychic intrusions.
- *Cedarwood* is an earthy oil that offers protection and grounding, anchoring one's energy while shielding against harm.

These oils are highly potent in their pure, undiluted form and should always be diluted with a carrier oil before being applied to the body. Recommended carrier oils include sweet almond oil, jojoba oil, fractionated coconut oil, and grapeseed oil. For every five millilitres (one teaspoon) of carrier oil, add two to three drops of essential oil. This prevents skin irritation or allergic reactions and ensures the oils blend safely with the energy field.

Once you know your skin tolerates it, you can increase the potency if needed. Importantly, always do a patch test before applying any oil blend to the body. Apply a small amount to the inner arm and wait twenty-four hours. Avoid contact with eyes, mucous membranes, or broken skin. Pregnant or breastfeeding women should consult a qualified practitioner first. Those with epilepsy, asthma, or high blood pressure should be especially cautious. Keep oils out of reach of children and pets.

Ritual: Drawing Protection Sigils with Oils

By drawing protection sigils with oils, you actively empower your body as a vessel of magick. These sacred markings act as your personal armour, warding off negativity and creating a space where only positive, protected energy may reside.

Needs

An oil of your choice for protection and an image of your choice for protection (e.g., a pentacle for powerful all-around protection, the Algiz rune for defence and safety, or a circle or spiral to create a protective boundary that deflects harmful energy).

Directions

Set your intention. Whether you're protecting yourself from psychic attacks, negative energies, or unwanted influences, focus your mind on this purpose.

Next, prepare your skin. Cleanse the area of the skin where you will draw the sigil. This could be your wrists, heart centre, or even your third eye. Ensure the skin is clear through a simple wash or a gentle cleansing ritual. Now, to draw the sigil, dip your finger or a small brush into the oil and draw your chosen protective symbol. Activate the sigil.

As you draw the symbol, focus on infusing the sigil with protective energy through the oil. Visualise it, creating a shield around your body, expanding outward to form an energetic barrier. Once the sigil is drawn, speak a short incantation to seal the protective energy by saying, "With this oil, this sigil I mark, a shield of light, no shadow shall dark. By skin and spirit, the ward is drawn, protected, I stand from dusk till dawn."

SACRED SMOKE FOR PURIFICATION

The sacred smoke of incense is often used to cleanse, purify, and protect people and their energies. Incense resins, drawn from the sap of trees, carry the potent energy of the earth and the spirit of the plant. Burning these resins releases their magickal properties, creating a protective veil of smoke that wards off negativity, harmful entities, and unwanted spirits. Whether burned during rituals or carried in sachets, these resins are powerful allies in magickal protection. Note that these same incenses can also work on spaces as well as the body.

- *Amber*—Shields against psychic attack; draws positive, protective energy into the home; and strengthens protective charms and amulets.
- *Benzoin*—Wards off evil spirits and negative influences, strengthens protective energy in rituals, and purifies the mind and spirit.
- *Copal*—Purifies and banishes negative energy, creates a protective boundary in sacred spaces, and is used to connect with ancestral spirits for protection.
- *Dragon's Blood*—Amplifies protective spells and rituals, banishes dark forces and negative energy, and creates a powerful shield around the home.
- *Frankincense*—Cleanses and purifies, wards off negative energy and harmful spirits, and strengthens spiritual protection during rituals.

- *Myrrh*—Protects against hexes and curses, shields against negative entities, and purifies and creates a sacred space.
- *Palo Santo*—Cleanses spaces and removes negative energy, protects the home from harmful entities, and grounds and strengthens protective rituals.
- *Pine Resin*—Cleanses and purifies spaces, protects against negative entities and energy, and grounds and strengthens personal protection.
- *Sandalwood*—Wards off negative spirits and harmful energies, protects during meditative and spiritual practices, and promotes peace while guarding against negativity.
- *Storax*—Protects against curses and banishes negativity, purifies spaces before rituals, and strengthens protective spells and talismans.

9
MAGICKAL CLOTHING AND TOOLS

Now that I've shared how to awaken the power within, it's time to explore how to extend this protective shield outward into the clothing you wear, the jewellery you adorn, and the tools you carry. Clothing, amulets, rings, and even the most straightforward tools can be powerful extensions of protective energy. Garments can be stitched with sacred symbols. Every piece of fabric can be enchanted, every stitch a spell. Likewise, amulets and talismans worn around the neck or placed in a pocket can radiate powerful protection. These physical tools serve as a bridge between the protective forces within you and the outer world. By wearing them, you anchor your magickal shield in the material realm, creating layers of defence that respond to the energies you encounter.

CHARMS

Charms are the personal talismans of a witch, infused with intention and magickal energy to guard and protect. Unlike wards, which often create boundaries in space, charms are portable protectors that can be carried on your person, placed in your home, or given to a loved one. These small but potent objects act as guardians, shielding their bearers from harm, negativity, or ill intent.

BASIC STEPS TO CREATE A PROTECTION CHARM

To create a charm, you must first gather the materials that resonate with the protective energies you wish to invoke. Herbs, crystals, and personal items can all serve as vessels for your magick, but your intention breathes life into them. When crafting a charm, carefully select each element, knowing its purpose is to protect.

For example, you might craft a protection pouch using black tourmaline for grounding, rosemary for purification, and a small personal item, such as a lock of hair or a photograph.

Place these items in a small cloth bag and, as you tie it closed, speak your intention. Try something simple like, "As I tie this charm, may it shield me from harm. By earth and sky, by flame and sea, let this charm protect me."

You can carry this charm, hang it above your door, or place it under your pillow for ongoing protection. I have crafted my ritual charm cord, which hangs on my belt around my waist and is infused with charms, herbs, staves, and lighting wood for protection.

JEWELLERY AS A CHARM

Jewellery can be a powerful protective charm. When enchanted with magickal intent, a ring, necklace, or bracelet can be a constant shield. Hold the piece of jewellery in your hands and focus on your intention. Visualise the energy of protection flowing from your heart and mind into the object, sealing it with your will.

For added power, you can anoint the jewellery with protective oils such as dragon's blood or frankincense while repeating a protective incantation, "With this oil, I seal my charm. May no ill touch me, may no harm draw near. This talisman protects me, strong and clear."

HERBAL CHARMS

You can create a charm by gathering protective herbs such as common sage, rosemary, or bay leaves. Wrap them in a cloth or bind them with a red string, creating a small bundle. These herb bundles can be hung in doorways, carried in a pocket, or placed in areas where protection is needed.

As you wrap the herbs, chant words of power, such as, "Sage for wisdom, rosemary for strength. By these herbs, I am protected at length." Herbal charms shield you and bring the earth's energy into your life, creating a natural barrier of protection.

ENCHANTMENT

Enchantment is the sacred act of imbuing an object with magickal energy and intent, transforming it into a powerful tool for protection. Unlike charms, which are often premade and filled with magickal ingredients, an enchanted object is brought to life through focused intention, becoming a living talisman that serves the witch in their craft. Enchantment can be woven into everyday objects, transforming the mundane into magickal protectors.

BASIC METHOD OF ENCHANTING OBJECTS

To enchant an object, you must first choose an item that resonates with your intention. This could be anything: jewellery, a stone, a wand, or a key. Once the object is chosen, enchantment begins with focus and will. Hold the object in your hands, feel its weight, and allow your energy to flow into it. Visualise a protective light surrounding the object, filling it to shield and guard.

As you breathe life into the object, speak words of power, such as, "By the light of the moon, by the strength of the sea, breathe into this tool the power to protect me. Through this enchantment, may it guard and defend; with my will, its power shall never end." With each word, you are weaving energy into the object, turning it from something simple into a potent protection tool.

ENCHANTING WITH THE ELEMENTS

You can call upon the elements to bless and charge the object to strengthen your enchantment. This deepens the connection between the magickal realm and the physical tool you are enchanting.

- *Earth:* Place the object in the soil or hold it with a grounding stone like obsidian or hematite. Call upon the earth to ground the object with strength and stability.
- *Air:* Pass the object through the smoke of incense or burning common sage to purify and charge it with clarity and wisdom.
- *Fire:* Briefly pass the object through the flame of a candle, invoking the element of fire to ignite the protective energy within it.

- *Water:* Sprinkle the object with blessed water or stormwater, calling upon the element of water to cleanse and empower the enchantment.

With these elemental blessings, the object is enchanted with your intent and the forces of nature, making it a truly powerful protector.

ENCHANTED CLOTHING AND ADORNMENTS

Whether you wear flowing robes under the moonlight or your everyday clothes, you can imbue them with magickal intent. With each stitch and fold, words of power are whispered, and protection energy is woven into the fabric. Choose colours that correspond to your protective intentions, such as black for warding, silver for psychic shielding, and gold for divine protection. What follows is a selection of the most common items of clothing and adornments.

- *Amulets and Talismans*—Perhaps the most powerful tools for daily protection are amulets and talismans. From enchanted rings and protective necklaces to carved stones and charms, these small yet mighty objects offer an ideal way to always carry protection with you.
- *Belt or Girdle*—The belt, wrapped around the waist, was seen as a barrier against lower vibrational forces. You can incorporate this practice into modern magick by inscribing protective symbols on the inside of your belt or girdle, creating a hidden layer of defence that travels with you. On my belt, I carry a blackthorn ward and a ritual cord with charms

representing my chosen deity, which hangs from my belt.

- *Necklaces*—Wearing a necklace close to your heart helps protect your emotional and spiritual core. Whether it holds a gemstone, a vial of protective herbs, or a sacred symbol like the pentacle or ankh, the energy radiating from your necklace creates a boundary of protection around your energy centres.
- *Rings*—A ring worn on the finger can act as a magickal shield. The ring's circular shape represents eternity and the unbroken cycle of protection. Choose stones like labradorite, black kyanite, and shungite to deflect negativity and psychic attacks.
- *Witch's Hat and Hood*—By charging their headwear with protection, the wearer envisions the hat or hood forming a protective dome around their aura. As a child in school, I was constantly put in the corner with the dunce's hat. However, I saw this hat as a cone of power, a way to harness my imagination as a witch. What the teachers saw as disempowerment, I saw as personal empowerment.

Think of it this way: Your inner power is your core, the magick within your body that fuels everything you do. Your clothing is your first layer of armour, wrapped around you to protect and ground your energy. Now, we move to the tools, each one a powerful conduit that allows you to project your magickal energy outward and create even stronger shields.

TOOLS OF PROTECTION

Magickal tools have always been an essential part of daily life, each carefully chosen to help focus energy and enhance protective spells. From the simple besom, used to sweep away negative energies, to the mighty staff planted in the earth to call upon elemental forces, these tools became extensions of power. You, too, can harness the protective power of these classic tools, each with its own energy and history. When combined with the protective magick we've cultivated within, they become powerful allies in your personal shield.

Whether you're using a wand to direct energy, a mirror to deflect negativity, or a bell to cleanse the air of unwanted spirits, these tools are as necessary to your protection as your clothing or inner magick. They are the final piece of the puzzle—the guardians that ensure no harmful force can breach the defences you've so carefully constructed. Here are the most important to consider.

ATHAME

The blade of boundaries, the athame is a ritual dagger that is not used for physical cutting but for energetically severing harmful connections and creating sacred space. It is used to cast circles, cut through negative energy, and protect the practitioner from malevolent forces.

BESOM

The sacred broom, the besom or broom sweeps away unwanted energies and clears a space of negativity. Used in ritual, it is a potent tool for cleansing and protecting the home. When hung above a doorway, it acts as a ward, preventing ill will from entering your space.

CAULDRON

Transformation of rebirth, the cauldron is a symbol of transformation and rebirth and serves as a powerful protective tool. Used to burn herbs, consecrate items, or hold sacred water, it absorbs and transmutes negative energies. Placed at the centre of your altar, it acts as a guardian of your space, amplifying protection spells and rituals.

CRYSTAL BALL

The watcher's eye, the crystal ball can act as a watchful eye beyond divination and help to detect and block harmful energies before they reach you. It can be placed on an altar as a protective beacon, filtering negativity from entering your space while keeping your awareness sharp.

GRIMOIRE OR BOOK OF SHADOWS

Keeper of secrets, your grimoire or Book of Shadows is a record of your magickal journey and a magickal tool in itself. Within its pages, spells, protective sigils, and rites are stored, guarded by the energy you imbue into them. When treated with respect, your book becomes a powerful protector of your knowledge and your space.

MIRRORS

In magickal protection, mirrors often reflect harmful energies, curses, or ill intentions back to their source. This ancient practice allows the mirror to act as a sentinel, standing guard and keeping negative forces at bay. A straightforward way to use mirror magick for protection is to hang a small mirror near your front door, facing outward. This will reflect any harmful energy trying to enter your home. You can also create a portable mirror charm by enchanting a small hand mirror to carry, ensuring that any negativity directed at you is reflected.

RED THREAD OR STRING

Red thread or string is woven into binding spells and charms for protection. Used to tie knots in protective rituals, symbolising the binding of harmful energy. Often worn or carried as a personal protective amulet.

STAFF

The ancient protector, the staff, taller and more grounded than the wand, is often used in outdoor rituals or as a walking stick on spiritual journeys. It represents strength and authority in the physical world, grounding protective energy into the earth while warding off unwanted spirits and energies.

STANG

The guardian of the crossroads, the stang, typically a forked staff, is a powerful tool for protection and crossing into other realms. It stands as a boundary marker in ritual space, creating a sacred division between the physical and spiritual worlds. As a protector, it holds the energy of both worlds and is often invoked to keep harmful spirits at bay.

WAND

The conductor of energy, the wand is a classic tool for directing and channelling energy. When used for protection, it helps focus your power, casting wards and shields with precision. Crafted from sacred wood or stone, it extends your will, cutting through negativity and creating protective barriers.

THE POWER FINGER

Also called the magickian's wand, the power finger is a potent tool in casting circles, a method deeply rooted in the personal magick that flows through your body. It is often referred to as the magickian's wand that is always with you, your index finger. By harnessing the energy from within and directing it outward through your power finger, you can channel your intention with precision and strength, drawing the protective boundary of a magickal circle with nothing more than the energy you already possess.

To enhance the effectiveness of your power finger, you can anoint it with a protective oil or trace symbols of strength and protection over it before casting. Some witches even tattoo symbols of power or protection on their index finger, making the tool even more potent. Your power finger isn't just for casting circles; it can also direct energy in many situations throughout your day. Whether drawing protective symbols in the air, charging your tools, or cleansing your space, your finger is an extension of your magick. By consciously using it, you deepen your connection to your energy, making it an integral part of your practice.

Ritual: Using the Power Finger for Casting Circles

In the same way we use wands or staves to cast, your power finger is a direct connection to the forces that reside within. The beauty of using the power finger is that it requires no additional tool, just you, your focus, and your intent.

Needs

Just you.

Directions

Before casting the circle, take a moment to ground yourself, feeling your connection to the earth beneath your feet and the energy flowing within you. Visualise this energy pooling in your core, ready to be released through your power finger.

As your power finger will serve as the conductor of energy, mentally align with the four elements. Imagine the earth beneath you providing stability, the air around you lending clarity, the fire within you fuelling your power, and the water that courses through your veins giving you fluidity and grace.

Now, with your power finger extended, begin walking clockwise around your space. As you do, visualise a trail of light flowing from your fingertip, leaving a shimmering circle of protection in its wake. This light could be a glowing blue, white, or any other colour that resonates with your intention. As you move, say, "By the power within me, I cast this circle. Earth, air, fire, and water, I call you forth. Let this space be sacred, shielded, and protected. It is done by the light of my hand and the will of my spirit." Finally, seal the circle. Draw the energy inward, visualising it tightening and solidifying the boundary. Touch your power finger to the ground and feel the energy lock in place, ensuring your circle is secure.

Part Two
THE WORK

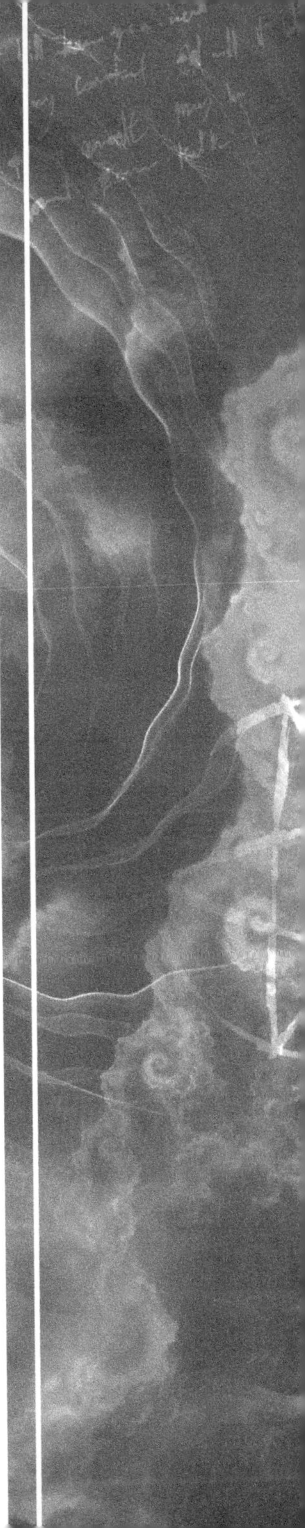

10
CRAFTING MAGICK

In the world of witchcraft, personalisation is the key to unlocking the full potential of your magick. No two witches' paths are the same, and the tools you work with should reflect your unique energy and intent. While traditional spells and rituals are powerful, their true strength comes alive when you infuse them with your essence.

Personalising your craft isn't just about creating tools, talismans, and other magickal items that look beautiful; it's about fostering a deeper connection between you, the materials you work with, and the magick you manifest.

SYMBOLIC SYMPATHY

Before the crafting begins, you should understand why you can foster that deep connection with the materials. Why does the magickal crafting work? In the sacred art of magick, symbolic sympathy is the thread that binds together unseen forces. It whispers that objects, symbols, and the energies they carry can mirror and influence one another, creating powerful ripples in the web of existence.

This time-tested principle lies at the heart of magickal protection, where symbols become shields and intent becomes the force that commands the spell.

Yet the intention—your pure, unwavering will—ignites the magick within. At the core of sympathetic magick, which fuels many protective workings, are two timeless laws: the Law of Similarity and the Law of Contagion.

THE LAW OF SIMILARITY

The poppet, for example, is lovingly crafted in a person's image and becomes their spiritual mirror. When you focus your intent on protection, you infuse that poppet with magickal strength, forming a shield around them. The poppet becomes their magickal guardian, reflecting your intention to keep them safe.

THE LAW OF CONTAGION

Once connected, always connected, as the law goes. An item that has touched your skin, hair, or clothing holds a part of you, an echo of your energy. By weaving these into your protection spells, you maintain that sacred link. Your intention guides the spell, ensuring that the energy follows the connection thread, surrounding you or your loved one in a circle of magickal defence.

* * *

These time-honoured laws are only as powerful as the intention you breathe into them. Without your focused will, the objects are mere tools waiting to be awakened. Your intention is the flame that kindles the protective energy, the force that shapes the magick. When you cast your circle, lay your stones, or light your candles, your heart's desire and focused mind powerfully charge these sacred symbols.

CHOOSING MATERIALS THAT RESONATE WITH YOU

The first step in personalising your craft is selecting the materials you work with—those that will help you foster that deep connection of sympathy. Whether you're crafting a poppet, a spell jar, or a talisman, the ingredients you choose should hold personal significance. This could be a favourite herb you've always been drawn to, a crystal that resonates with your energy, or even a colour that carries a specific meaning.

STEP ONE: CHOOSE YOUR MATERIALS

At its core, witchcraft is a deeply personal practice. Your energy flows into every tool, charm, and ritual you create. By selecting materials that resonate with you, imbuing objects with your energy, and aligning your tools with your unique intentions, you transform simple items into powerful conduits for protection and empowerment.

For example, suppose you feel a strong connection to the element of fire. You might incorporate red candles, fire agate crystals, or fiery herbs like cinnamon or cayenne pepper into your protective work. If you're more attuned to the earth, grounding stones like hematite or herbs like common sage and patchouli might resonate with your personal energy. The key is to trust your intuition and select powerful materials that align with your purpose.

Incorporating personal items such as a lock of your hair, a piece of jewellery, or a handwritten intention can further deepen the connection between the tool and your energy. These items carry your unique vibration, making the magick you cast even more potent. Including these personal items in your tools creates an unbreakable bond between your energy and your magickal work.

STEP TWO: INFUSING YOUR ENERGY INTO YOUR CRAFT

Once you've selected your materials, the next step is to infuse them with your energy. This process transforms ordinary objects into magickal tools, linking them directly to your will and intention. To do this, you can hold the item in your hands, close your eyes, and visualise the energy flowing from your body into the object. See the object glowing with the energy you are imbuing into it.

As you infuse your tools with energy, speak aloud your intention for their use. For example, you might say, "I charge this crystal with the power to protect my home" or "I bless this herb with the strength to ward off negative energy." The spoken word is a powerful tool in witchcraft, and by voicing your intention, you give life to your magickal protection.

Another way to personalise your craft is through ritual. You can anoint your tools with oils, pass them through smoke, or leave them under the full moon's light to charge them with energy. Consecrating your tools purifies and aligns them with your vibration, making them powerful extensions of your magick.

STEP THREE: ALIGN WITH YOUR INTENTIONS

Personalising your craft is not only about the physical supplies but also about aligning your energy and intent with the magick you wish to create. This means being aware of your intentions before you begin any spell or ritual. Meditate on what you want to achieve, visualising your desired outcome. The stronger and more focused your intention, the more powerful your magick will be. When you personalise your magick this way, you work with the universe's energy and draw upon your inner power. This alignment of self and intention is the heart of personal magick; it sets your practice apart from others and allows you to weave unique spells and protections.

STEP FOUR: ADD SYMBOLS AND SIGILS

One powerful way to personalise your craft is by incorporating symbols and sigils. These visual representations of your intention can be carved into candles, drawn on spell jars, or even traced in the air with your fingers. Creating your sigils allows you to encode your desires into the fabric of your magick.

STEP FIVE: ADD YOUR MAGICKAL SIGNATURE

As you continue to personalise your craft, you may find certain symbols, materials, or rituals become part of your magickal signature, an energetic blueprint unique to you. This signature is the essence of your practice, a reflection of your power and how you work with magickal forces. Your magickal signature can be woven into everything you do, from the herbs you use to how you cast a circle. It is an expression of your individuality as a witch, and as you grow in your practice, it will become more refined and distinct. This makes your magick uniquely yours, imbued with only the power and energy you can bring.

STEP SIX: EMBRACE YOUR INTUITION

Above all, personalising your craft is about trusting your intuition. Magick is a fluid, ever-evolving practice, and the more you listen to your inner voice, the more powerful your work will become. If a specific herb calls to you, even if it's not traditionally used in protection spells, trust there's a reason. Your intuition is one of the most potent tools in your arsenal, and by following its guidance, you will create a magick that is genuinely personal and deeply aligned with your spirit.

When you personalise your craft, you are not simply following instructions; you are crafting a unique, powerful form of magick that resonates with your soul. Every spell, tool, and ritual becomes an extension of your will, reflecting your personal power and connection to the universe. As we create a magickal crafting altar, remember that your craft is yours. By personalising your tools, rituals, and intentions, you are forging a unique path filled with the magick only you can create.

YOUR MAGICKAL ALTAR

A magickal crafting altar is the heart of your creative and protective work. It is a dedicated space to infuse your tools, materials, and intentions with focused energy. This sacred space is a personal haven, allowing you to fully immerse yourself in your craft while drawing upon the elemental and spiritual forces that guide your magickal work.

Location is critical when setting up a magickal crafting altar. Choose a space to work uninterrupted and feel connected to your magick. Whether indoors or outdoors, it's essential that this area resonates with you and feels sacred. Begin by purifying the space using incense, salt, or water to remove any lingering energy that may interfere with your crafting.

The altar itself can be as simple or elaborate as you wish. A cloth representing protection, such as deep blue or black, can be laid out to form a base. At the centre, place a candle, which will serve as the focal point of your work, igniting the flame of your intention. Surround it with essential tools, such as your athame, wand, chalice, and protective symbols or statues of deities with which you feel a connection. Herbs, crystals, and oils used for crafting magickal tools should also be kept nearby.

For protection work, consider adding items that are precisely aligned with protective energy. A bowl of sea salt or protective herbs such as mountain sage and rosemary can help fortify the space. Crystals like labradorite or fluorite will help maintain a shield of spiritual defence. Sacred objects, such as personal talismans or amulets, can be placed on the altar to further enhance their protective power.

As you craft, allow your altar to be a living, breathing extension of your magick. Feel the energy build each time you return to it, deepening your connection to the unseen forces that guide and protect you. Consecrate your tools here, blessing each one with the power of protection and intention. This altar is more than a place to create; it is where you forge sacred bonds, drawing strength from the energies you invite into your space.

One of my most cherished memories of Granny Winnie is how she infused magick into everyday objects, like her witch's spoons. These weren't just simple kitchen tools; they were powerful charms used in folk magick to bring protection, abundance, and blessings into the home.

Crafted carefully, each spoon was carved with protective symbols or tied with coloured ribbons, serving a dual purpose. In the kitchen, they stirred intentions into meals, while those hung in windows or doorways acted as silent guardians, protecting the home from negativity.

You can carry forward the same tradition as you work at your altar. Just as Granny Winnie did with her spoons, she transformed simple objects into something with purpose. Whether it's a spoon hanging in your window or a tool consecrated on your altar, each becomes a vessel for your magick, a living charm that brings your intentions into the physical world.

In this way, your home becomes a protective space filled with the everyday magick witches have used for generations. I still remember the warmth and safety those spoons brought into her home. They were more than just a tradition; they were a daily reminder of the power of simple, everyday crafting magick.

CANDLE MAGICK

Candle magick is one of the simplest yet most effective forms of protection crafting in witchcraft. The flame of a candle represents the element of fire, a powerful force that can burn away negativity, shield against harm, and illuminate the path of safety. When used with intention, candles become conduits for protective energy, creating barriers and warding off harmful forces.

CHOOSING THE RIGHT CANDLES

Selecting the right candle for your protection work is more than just choosing a colour; it's about aligning every aspect of the candle with your specific intention. Black candles are most used for general protection because they absorb and banish negative energy. White candles can purify and create a shield of light around you, while red candles ignite protective passion and energy, especially during urgent situations.

Beyond colour, the size and shape of the candle can also be important. Larger pillar candles can provide sustained protection over time, while small votive or tealight candles are perfect for quick, targeted rituals. You can also work with figure candles, such as a candle shaped like a person, to protect yourself or another person.

CREATING YOUR CANDLE SPELL

To enhance the power of your candle, it's essential to prepare and dress it before beginning your ritual. Start by carving protective symbols, runes, or sigils directly into the wax, imbuing the candle with your specific intention. Whether you carve a simple pentacle, a rune of protection like Algiz, or a personalised sigil, inscribing the candle aligns it with your will. Next, dress the candle with protective oils such as rosemary, frankincense, or cedarwood. Gently anoint the candle with oil, stroking upward to invoke protective energy or downward to banish negativity. You can also roll the candle in protective herbs, such as basil, bay leaves, or mugwort to further strengthen its protective power.

Once the candle is dressed and prepared, the ritual becomes a dance between you and the flame. Light the candle with intention, speaking your purpose aloud as the flame ignites. As the candle burns, visualise the flame, creating a protective barrier around you, the person, or the space you wish to shield. Feel the warmth of the flame growing, expanding outward, pushing away harm, and creating a space of safety. For more targeted protection, place the candle on your altar or in a room that requires guarding. Allow the candle to burn down completely, sealing the protection with the final flicker of the flame.

BANISHMENT WITH CANDLE MAGICK

Candle magick is equally practical when protecting and banishing harmful energies or influences. Black candles are potent tools for banishment, absorbing negative energy and neutralising threats. As with protection, carve banishing symbols or sigils into the wax, dress the candle with banishing oils such as patchouli or dragon's blood, and burn it while focusing on removing harmful energy from your life. As the candle burns, visualise the flame dissolving and clearing away all negativity, leaving only peace and safety behind.

OTHER PROTECTION CRAFTS

When creating any spell, the most crucial element is your intent, what you wish to protect, and how you wish to protect it. The process is a ritual, combining aspects of nature and spirit to create something magickal.

POPPETS

Poppets, also known as witch dolls, are one of the most versatile tools in witchcraft. These handmade figures serve as stand-ins for a person or situation, allowing the witch to focus energy, intent, and magick on the target they represent. Poppets have been crafted from natural materials like cloth, straw, clay, or roots, with each material contributing its unique energy to the spell. These dollies can safeguard an individual, space, or situation in protection magick. The key is to infuse the poppet with intent; whether you're protecting a loved one, yourself, or a place, the poppet becomes a vessel for protective energy.

CREATING A POPPET

The creation process is sacred and personal. You stick or mould your poppet and, as you do, visualise it absorbing your intentions. Once crafted, the poppet can be filled with protective herbs, crystals, or personal items, such as hair or clothing, to strengthen its connection to the target. Herbs like bay leaves, angelica (*Angelica archangelica*), or mugwort are potent choices for protection. For crystals, consider using smoky quartz to dissipate negative energy, amethyst for spiritual protection, or lapis lazuli to enhance communication with spiritual guides. The poppet can be placed in a sacred space, hidden in a home, or carried with you for ongoing protection.

To enhance the poppet's potency, you may carve protective symbols into it or dress it in specific colours associated with protection, such as black, red, or white. The true power of the poppet lies in its ability to bridge the material and spiritual realms, allowing witches to focus their energy and intentions on a physical object. When appropriately crafted and empowered, poppets serve as powerful guardians, defending against harm and offering protection magick wherever needed.

WITCHES' BALLS

Witches' balls are ancient protective charms that ward off negative energies, malicious spirits, and harmful influences. Traditionally made from glass and hung in windows or doorways, witches' balls are often filled with herbs, crystals, and other magickal items to amplify their protective powers.

CREATING A WITCHES' BALL

To create your own witches' ball, choose a glass ball, which can be clear or coloured depending on your intention. Traditionally, reflective surfaces are said to deflect negative energy, but you can choose what resonates with you. Once you have your ball, it's time to fill it with protective items. Add dried herbs like rosemary, lavender, or mugwort for protection and purification. Then, add tiny crystals, choosing from tourmaline, amethyst, or obsidian. Select a feather for spiritual protection or add a thorn to ward off intruders or harmful influences and a pinch of salt to absorb negativity and purify the space.

After filling your witches' ball with your chosen items, hang it near a window, door, or central point in your home. As it hangs, it will act as a guardian, protecting your space by deflecting and trapping harmful energy. You can also charge your witches' ball under the moonlight or with a protective incantation to amplify its power. Over time, your witches' ball may absorb and trap a significant amount of negative energy. It's essential to renew and cleanse it periodically. You can maintain potency by removing the items inside, washing the ball with smoke or salt water, and refilling it with fresh herbs and crystals.

WITCH'S LADDER

The witch's ladder is a powerful knot magick that binds protective energy into an object. Traditionally, this magick involves braiding or tying cords and incorporating feathers, beads, or small charms into the knots. Each knot represents a specific intention, often tied with words of power, to form a protective shield.

CREATING A WITCH'S LADDER

To create a witch's ladder for protection, braid three cords together, tying in small objects such as black feathers for banishing negativity or beads to amplify your intent. With each knot, say, "By knot of one, the spell's begun. By knot of two, protection is true. By knot of three, harm shall not be." Once completed, the witch's ladder can be hung in your home or carried as a constant ward against harm.

AMULETS AND TALISMANS

Throughout history, those who work with magick have relied on the power of amulets and talismans to shield themselves and others from harm. Though often used interchangeably, there is a subtle difference between the two. Amulets are natural or crafted objects imbued with protective energy, designed to guard the wearer from hostile forces. Conversely, talismans are specifically crafted to attract power, good fortune, or a particular kind of energy, such as protection, to the bearer. Both are powerful allies in the art of magickal defence.

CRAFTING AN AMULET OF PROTECTION

Amulets often come from nature's bounty—stones, crystals, herbs, bones, or wood, each carrying its inherent energy. To craft an amulet, select a natural object that resonates with your intention for protection. This could be a protective black tourmaline, a sprig of rosemary, or even a seashell that speaks to you. Allow your intuition to guide you as you choose the object that will become your amulet.

Once selected, the amulet must be cleansed and consecrated. Cleanse it with smoke from protective herbs, such as sage or cedar (*Cedrus atlantica*), or bathe it in salt water to purify it of any prior energies. As you cleanse, focus on your intention and imagine the amulet absorbing the power to protect and guard. To further empower the amulet, you can carve or paint a protective symbol or sigil on its surface.

Whether it's a pentacle, the rune of Algiz, or a personal sigil crafted for protection, this mark becomes a beacon of your will, enhancing the amulet's energy. Once consecrated, the amulet can be worn, carried, or placed in a sacred space. It constantly works to protect you or your home. It becomes a living shield, charged with your intention and the power of the natural world.

CRAFTING A TALISMAN FOR PROTECTION

Unlike an amulet, which often comes from natural elements, a talisman is usually created from scratch, specifically designed to channel protective energy. Talismans can be crafted from a variety of materials, including metal, cloth, or any other suitable material.

To begin, select a material that resonates with the level of protection you seek. Silver is often used for psychic protection, while iron is believed to ward off evil spirits. Once you've chosen your material, craft the talisman by engraving or inscribing protective symbols, runes, or sigils onto its surface. You may wish to include words of power or names of deities, guardians, or spirits with whom you feel a connection. These marks act as anchors, binding the talisman to its protective purpose.

The next step is to empower the talisman. This can be achieved through ritual, utilising fire, water, earth, or air to imbue it with the energy of the elements. Hold the talisman and speak your intention aloud, calling on the protection forces to reside within it. You can also incorporate candle magick, allowing a black or white candle to burn as you focus on infusing the talisman with your magick.

Once crafted and empowered, the talisman becomes a vessel of concentrated magickal energy. It can be carried on your person, placed on an altar, or kept in your home, constantly attracting protective forces and warding off harm. Like an amulet, it grows stronger with time, becoming a trusted companion in your magickal practice.

Both amulets and talismans are potent tools in witchcraft. They offer continuous protection and empower you to walk through the world with confidence and magick at your side. The key lies in the intent and ritual you pour into them, transforming simple objects into powerful shields against harm.

SPELL JARS AND BOTTLES

Spell jars and bottles have long been used in witchcraft to contain and focus protective energy. These small yet powerful containers become homes for the magick we craft, acting as a continuous shield against harmful forces.

CREATING A PROTECTIVE SPELL JAR

When crafting a protection jar, begin with a small glass bottle or jar. Choose black pepper (*Piper nigrum*) to ward off negativity, thorns for added defence, or an evil eye charm to reflect harm to its source. As you place each item in the jar, speak your intent clearly, empowering the object with your voice. To amplify its power, choose onyx for grounding protection or tiger's eye for shielding against psychic attacks. Once filled, the spell jar becomes a personal guardian, working continuously to keep you safe from harm.

The next crucial step is sealing the jar. Use wax to seal the top, choose a candle colour that matches the intention: black for banishment, white for purification, or red for energetic protection. As the wax drips over the jar, visualise the protective energy within being locked in place, creating a powerful boundary between you and any threat. Speak words of power or a protective incantation as you seal the jar, binding the energy to your will.

Where you store the jar for its life matters; keeping it near your front door or windows protects against external threats, and placing it on your altar allows it to absorb protective energies during rituals. If personal protection is your goal, carry a smaller version with you in a bag or pocket.

YOUR WITCH'S SHIELD

We'll end with a protective magickal craft that needs no tools or supplies. The witch's shield is your magickal boundary, a spell of protection woven into your daily life. Whether you're walking through a crowded city, scrolling through your phone, or dealing with the emotions of those around you, the witch's shield stands between you and the energies that wish to intrude. It's a quiet yet powerful force that ensures you remain grounded, untouched by the chaos that moves through the world.

This shield doesn't just guard against external threats; it strengthens your magick. When your energy is protected, your spells become clearer, your intuition sharper, and your connection to the elements more potent. The witch's shield protects and empowers, making it a vital tool for every modern witch.

By casting your witch's shield, you declare sovereignty over your energy. You claim your power and set a clear boundary that no harmful force may cross. The witch's shield will ensure that you stand firm, centred, and protected in your magickal practice.

CREATING YOUR WITCH'S SHIELD

When you cast your witch's shield, envision yourself standing as the shield maiden did—strong, grounded, and surrounded by a powerful circle of protection. Feel the shield's energy around you as an impenetrable wall, reflecting negativity, deflecting harm, and standing as your sacred defence. Breathe in the essence of the shield, letting it form around you, shimmering with magickal energy. Feel your protection magick surrounding you, strong and steadfast.

11
SEALS, SIGILS, SYMBOLS, AND WORDS

There is an ancient current of power that runs beneath the visible world, and seals, sigils, symbols, and words are the bridges that allow us to tap into it. These are the sacred tools of the witch, not merely representations but active forces that shape energy, command spirits, and speak to the universe in the language it remembers. A symbol, when charged with intention, becomes a living spell. A sigil, birthed from a focused will, is a portal through which your desire passes into manifestation. Seals hold authority over seen and unseen realms, often linked to spirits, daemons, or divine intelligence. And words—spoken, whispered, or written—are incantations that reverberate through the web of creation, altering the fabric of reality. This is not fantasy. This is the forgotten science of the soul, the occult architecture that underpins all magick.

For me, the journey began at five years old when I first drew a triple spiral—the Triskelion.

I didn't know its name, only that it had come from somewhere deep within. That symbol became my first key, unlocking something ancient in my blood. It called me to the sacred places of the earth, where stones still hum with forgotten rites. My first pilgrimage was to Newgrange, where the carved spiral outside the mound mirrored the one I had drawn years before. Standing before it, I felt an intense remembrance stir—of lives lived, wisdom kept, and symbols used to mark portals between worlds. From that moment, I understood that these signs are not passive but alive. They are sigils of sovereignty, maps of the magickal cosmos, and echoes of the witch's eternal voice.

MAGICKAL SEALS

Magickal seals are age-old symbols used to invoke protection, power, and divine guidance. They are placed on doors and windows or inscribed on tools and amulets to enhance protective power. You can also draw inspiration from traditional magickal seals such as the sigil of Saturn for protection or Solomonic seals, used in ceremonial magick, to shield and control spiritual forces. Magickal seals can be used in various ways. You can inscribe them on the corners of your home for protection, draw them in the air during rituals, or place them on objects like talismans and spell jars.

Seals can also be carved into candles to enhance their power during protection rituals. Remember, the seal holds the energy of your intention and the forces you've called upon. Regularly cleansing and recharging the seal ensures it remains a potent tool for your magickal protection.

CREATING YOUR MAGICKAL SEAL

To begin crafting your seal, consider the specific type of protection you are seeking. Is it protection from negative energy, psychic attacks, or harmful spirits? Once your intent is clear, you can design your seal from scratch or use one with historical or mystical significance.

Select symbols, runes, or geometric shapes that align with your purpose when creating a seal from scratch. For example, a circle can represent a protective boundary, while triangles may invoke strength and stability. Combine these elements into a unique seal that resonates with your intention.

Once your seal is created, activating and empowering it is essential. This can be done through a simple ritual. Begin by placing the seal on your altar or in a sacred space. Light a candle for protection, preferably a black or white candle, and focus your energy on the seal. Visualise a glowing light surrounding it, imbuing it with protective energy. Declare the purpose of the seal by saying, "By the power of the elements and the forces that guard, I consecrate this seal for protection, that it may shield me from harm and reflect all negativity away." You may also anoint the seal with protective oils such as frankincense or dragon's blood to enhance its power. Once activated, the seal can be placed on doors and windows or carried with you for constant protection.

SIGILS

In addition to ancient symbols, sigils are powerful tools in modern witchcraft, deeply woven into the practice of protection. A sigil is a unique symbol created with intention, designed to embody your will in a visual form. These custom glyphs act as direct channels for your magickal energy, making them incredibly personal and effective for protection.

CREATING A SIGIL

To create a sigil, begin by formulating a clear intention, such as "I am protected." Break the phrase down by removing any repeating letters and combining the remaining ones into a unique, intricate design. This is the weaving of your will into a symbol. Once crafted, charge your sigil by focusing on it during meditation by the light of a candle or by using the elements to empower it.

When the sigil is charged with your energy, it can be drawn on doorways, carved into candles, or inscribed on talismans to protect you and your space continually. Like ancient symbols, sigils transcend the material world and connect to the hidden realms of energy, offering a personal and potent way to protect yourself through the art of witchcraft.

PROTECTIVE SYMBOLS

Throughout the ages, witches have turned to symbols to invoke powerful protection. Each symbol carries its unique energy, and when drawn, carved, or worn, these glyphs become living shields that guard against harm. Whether it's the ancient pentacle or the intricate spiral of the Triskelion, these symbols have been used for centuries, guiding us in the art of protection.

Personally, I love working with protective symbols. I've explored many traditions and ancient drawings, from the Triskelion's whirling power to the timeless knotwork of the witch's knot. Each one teaches us something new about the deeper magick of protection. These symbols speak across the ages, offering us strength and wisdom as we weave their energy into our craft. Here is a list of twenty symbols. Enjoy discovering how to work with each one within your crafting.

OCCULT AND WITCHCRAFT PROTECTIVE SYMBOLS

Algiz (Rune of Protection)

Bindrune of Protection

Blackthorn Cross

Crossroads Symbol

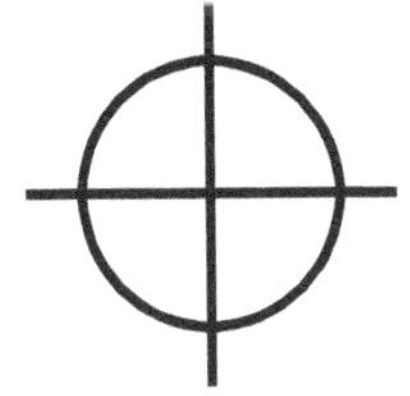

The Dragon's Eye

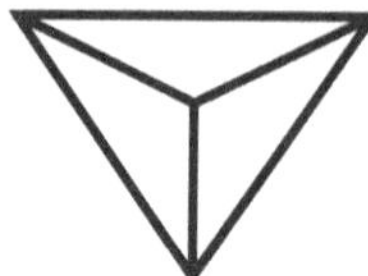

Eye of Providence

Four Elements Symbols

Hexagram

The Horned God Symbol

Key of Solomon

Ouroboros

Pentacle

The Shield Knot

Sigil of Saturn

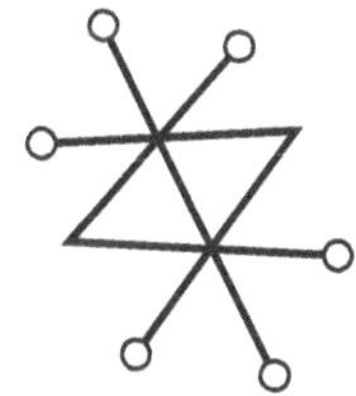

The Solar Cross

Triple Moon

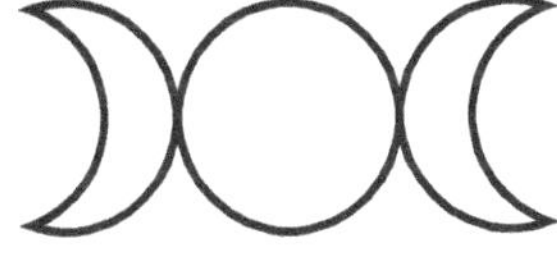

Triskelion

Witch's Knot

CREATING PROTECTIVE SYMBOLS

While many ancient symbols offer powerful protection, magick is deeply personal, and you can create your own symbols to serve as guardians. By combining your intent with the act of creation, you weave protection into each unique glyph you craft.

As a young child, I drew spirals without knowing why. It was a symbol that felt natural and powerful in my hands. Years later, when I visited Newgrange in Ireland, I was struck by the triple spiral, the Triskelion, carved into the stones at the entrance.

This ancient symbol of protection left a deep impression on me; I had always known its power long before seeing it in the flesh. The experience reminded me that the symbols we feel connected to often have deeper meanings, and sometimes we carry the wisdom of ancient magick within us, waiting to be unlocked. I encourage you to create protective symbols guided by your intuition and the magick within you. When imbued with intention, these personal glyphs can become as powerful as ancient ones.

INCANTATIONS

Words are made up of letters, which are symbols of sounds. Together they have meaning. When we speak or chant these words in different ways, we create vibrations that influence the energies around us. The voice becomes a conduit for magick, with each word resonating outward, carrying our will into the universe. Speaking aloud sharpens focus, clarifying our intentions.

The more precise the words, the more potent the protection. And by speaking words of power, we connect to the ancient tradition of spellcraft. Speaking magickal words aligns us with the ancients, drawing on the collective strength of those who walked the path before us.

CREATING YOUR PROTECTIVE INCANTATION

Before crafting your protective incantation, it is essential to consider the following: Be clear about what you are asking for and protect yourself from specific energies, situations, or individuals.

Try creating a cadence when you speak, whether it's a chant, rhyme, or repetitive phrasing. Invoke specific deities, such as Ra or Heka, who offer protection. By naming them in your incantation, you call upon their ancient power to assist you in your work.

HOW TO USE AN INCANTATION

Create a sacred space by lighting a candle. Stand in a position of power, feet planted firmly on the ground, arms extended, or hands raised in an invoking posture. Focus your energy on the intention of protection. Recite the incantation aloud, allowing the words to vibrate through the space.

Speak with conviction and authority, knowing that the words you release carry the power to manifest protection. For added strength, you can repeat the incantation three times, raising your voice slightly with each repetition to build energy. When the incantation is complete, feel the energy shift around you. Seal the incantation with the phrase, "By the circle's power and ancient decree, it is sealed."

A PROTECTIVE INCANTATION INSPIRED BY THE EGYPTIAN PRIESTHOOD

Here is a crafted incantation based on the ancient rites of the Egyptian temple priests. It can invoke the protective energies of Ra and Heka, drawing their power to shield you in times of need.

By the light of Ra, the sun that never fades, I call upon your strength, your eternal blaze. Wrap me in your fiery shield, pure and bright, guard me through the day and watch me through the night. By the power of Heka, a magickal force divine, I summon the unseen threads through space and time. Weave a shield of energy, strong and true, let no ill intention pass through.

I speak these words with power and might, let them ripple through the realms of light. By ancient decree and the gods' command, I am protected by my voice; I stand. Ra, grant me the flame to burn away fear; Heka, weave the veil that none may pierce here. By the gods of old, my path is sealed, in solar, fire and magick are revealed. So it is spoken, so it is done, protected by the moon and sun. Amun.

12
THE SPIRIT OF THE HOME

The first time I truly felt the presence of a house spirit, it was as though I had stepped into an ancient embrace, a presence that wrapped around me like the warmth of a familiar cloak. Homes are more than just brick and mortar; they are living, breathing entities imbued with the echoes of all who have dwelled within their walls. Over the years, I've lived in many different homes, ranging from quaint stone cottages nestled deep in the countryside to towering city apartments that stretch into the sky. Each space carried its unique energy, a distinct hum that spoke of the lives and experiences that had unfolded within it. But none of these places stirred the depths of my soul like the moment I crossed the threshold of the home I now inhabit, perched above our magickal shop in Buxton.

This home felt different, alive, pulsing with a deep, quiet wisdom. It had a soul, a guardian spirit that stirred the air with whispers, as if acknowledging and recognising me. The energy wasn't just welcoming; it was protective, wrapping around me like a cloak of belonging, offering comfort, safety, and magick in equal measure. From that moment, I knew that this house held more than just the energy of those who had come before. It carried the essence of the land beneath it, the ancient stones of the hills surrounding it, and the power of the earth that had cradled it for centuries.

Each house has its own story and spirit, woven from the emotions, thoughts, and intentions of the lives that pass through its doors. Every smile, every tear, whispered secret, and every spoken word leaves an imprint, an energetic fingerprint that lingers long after the people have gone. But this house was something different. Its spirit was ancient, steady, and wise. It felt like it had been watching over the space for lifetimes, long before my feet touched its floors. It wasn't just about the energy within its walls; it was about the soul that resided deep within the heart of this home.

I felt it immediately as if the guardian spirit of the house had been waiting for me, recognising my energy as someone who would not only live within its walls but also care for and honour its spirit. From that moment, I knew that my relationship with this house would be one of mutual respect, a sacred partnership of guardianship. I was not just living in this house; I had become part of its story, heartbeat, and magick. This was not just a shelter from the elements; it was a living, breathing sanctuary, a space of magick and protection that would grow and thrive alongside me.

Since that fateful day, I have woven the house's spirit into my daily rituals. Each time I cross the threshold, I take a moment to pause, to breathe deeply, and to connect with the spirit of the house. I greet it with the ringing of a small brass bell that hangs by the door, a sound that resonates through the air and stirs the energies around me. The chime is a signal, a declaration of my return, an acknowledgement of the guardian that watches over this sacred space. The bell's gentle tones ripple through the air, harmonising with the ancient essence within the walls. It's a simple but powerful gesture, one that reinforces the bond I have with this place.

When I leave, I ring the bell again, a sound that lingers, echoing softly as I step out into the world. At this moment, I ask the spirit of the house to watch over the space in my absence, to keep it safe and shielded from any harm that may attempt to enter. It is a quiet, sacred exchange, one built on trust, respect, and a deep understanding of the house's protective power. The ringing of the bell has become as natural to me as breathing, a daily ritual that strengthens the invisible thread of magick that ties me to this space.

Over time, I have come to realise that the spirit of a home is not static. It grows and shifts, responding to the energies within and around it. Just as we cleanse and nurture our spirits, so must we care for the spirit of our home. Through small, daily acts of magick, we can honour the guardian spirit that protects and nourishes the space, ensuring that it remains a place of balance, harmony, and safety.

In this chapter, I will guide you through the sacred art of connecting with the spirit of your home. Together, we will explore how to fortify your home's boundaries, cleanse its energy, and invoke protective forces to shield it from harm. Whether you are just beginning your journey into home protection or deepening your existing practices, the wisdom of the house spirit will guide you as you weave your magickal bond with the space you call home.

A house is far more than just the sum of its physical parts. When we open ourselves to its energy and honour the spirit that dwells within, we transform it into a sanctuary—a place of magick, protection, and peace. Let this chapter be your guide as we walk together through the sacred act of home protection, calling upon ancient wisdom to protect and empower the space where you rest, dream, and thrive.

THE LIVING THRESHOLD

The threshold is a place of profound power where two worlds meet: The outer realm of chaos, filled with the unpredictable energies of the world beyond, and the inner sanctuary of peace, where you weave your magick and nurture your spirit. Here, at the doorway, the veil between the mundane and the mystical is at its thinnest. The threshold is not merely a passage but the first line of defence, the sacred boundary between the world outside and the sanctum within. To leave this portal unguarded is to allow discord to slip into your space unnoticed and to disrupt the delicate balance of peace and protection you've so carefully cultivated.

Remember that a threshold is a living thing, a space of constant motion and energy exchange. Every time you cross it, you interact with the magick you've woven there. Please take a moment to pause as you step across it, whether entering or leaving. Feel the protective energy that surrounds you and honour the boundary that keeps your inner sanctuary safe from the chaos beyond.

BASIC THRESHOLD PROTECTION

A common magickal practice is to use colours to fortify your doorway. Painting the door in protective hues such as red, purple, or black is a potent way to signal to the world that your home is a sanctuary—a place of strength and protection. Red is the colour of vitality, fire, and courage, while black absorbs and neutralises negativity, and purple is associated with witchcraft and protection. Consider painting your door in one of these colours or drawing protective symbols such as a pentacle or rune around the frame. Each time you open or close the door, take a moment to silently acknowledge the protection these colours and symbols provide, reinforcing your intention with each action.

Additionally, you can etch or paint sigils of protection onto the inside of the doorframe or above the lintel. Infused with your intent, these sigils act as permanent guardians, silently watching over your threshold. As you trace the sigil, say, "By this mark, this door is sealed. By my will, no harm revealed."

Ritual: Guarding Your Threshold

Do the following ritual whenever you need to refresh or strengthen the magick at your threshold. Just as the tides of energy ebb and flow, so must we tend to the protective barriers we set. In this ritual, you will use salt, which is revered as a potent protector as it absorbs negativity and guards against unwanted forces. Whether through a simple sweep of your besom, the refreshing of moon water, or the anointing of oil, remember that each action strengthens the veil between your home and the outside world, ensuring that your space remains a sanctuary of peace, protection, and magick.

Needs

A broom or besom, blackthorn salt, a protective token such as a horseshoe (luck and protection), a pentacle (strength), and a bundle of protective herbs tied with red thread (rosemary, common sage, and lavender).

Directions

Begin by cleansing the space with reverence, acknowledging that you are not simply sweeping away dust but banishing the energies that no longer serve you. Take up your besom, your sacred broom, consecrated for magickal work, and begin at the back of your home, sweeping your way toward the front door. With each stroke, envision all stagnant and negative energy being collected, swept up in the bristles, and guided out of your home. Picture the energy as a dull fog pushed away by the sweeping motion, gradually revealing the glowing light of protection beneath.

As you near the door, feel the shift in the air. The threshold awaits your magick, ready to be sealed and fortified. When you reach the front door, sprinkle a line of salt across the threshold. As the salt falls, declare, "By salt and sweep, I guard this door. No harm may enter; no darkness anymore." The salt acts as a barrier, a line in the sand that no malevolent force can cross without being purified and neutralised. It is the first layer of your magickal defence, but more layers await.

Next, turn your attention to the energy above and around the doorway. Every threshold should carry a charm, a token of magick imbued with intent. Whether you chose a horseshoe for luck and protection, a pentacle for strength, or the bundle of protective herbs, imbue it with your intent. Hold it and know that this charm is a guardian in its own right, holding fast against harmful energies. Hang it near your threshold.

As you hang your charm above the doorframe, feel its magick stir and hum. Speak these words of power: "By herb and iron, by spirit and light, this door is sealed, protected by night."

SMOKE CLEANSING SPACE

Saining, a traditional Scottish practice of smoke cleansing, is a powerful form of purification and protection. Used for centuries to ward off evil spirits, negative energy, and harmful influences, saining invokes the protective power of herbs through sacred smoke. Unlike other forms of smoke cleansing, saining is deeply rooted in the Celtic tradition, connecting the practitioner to the ancient energies of the land and its spirits.

My first encounter with saining came under the guidance of Swein, one of my earliest mentors in magickal protection. As a teenager, I remember standing in the cool air of the Highlands, watching as Swein lit the dried herbs, letting the smoke rise and drift through the air. With each movement, he explained the importance of intention and his specific herbs: juniper (*Juniperus communis*) for protection, rowan (*Sorbus aucuparia*) for strength, and heather (*Culluna vulgaris*) for peace.

He showed me how to use the smoke to cleanse a space, sweeping it through doorways and around the perimeter to create a boundary no ill intent could cross. Swein's teachings instilled in me the sacredness of this ritual, and to this day, it remains one of my most cherished methods of protection magick. Here's a short list of the herbs used in saining with their properties:

- ***Heather*** (*Calluna vulgaris*) promotes peace and calm, provides gentle protection for emotional well-being, and attracts positive, healing energy while dispelling negativity.
- ***Juniper*** (*Juniperus communis*) wards off negative energy and evil spirits, provides strong protection for the home and personal space, and purifies and cleanses harmful influences.
- ***Rowan*** (*Sorbus aucuparia*) protects against enchantment and dark magick, strengthens psychic shields and barriers, and wards off malevolent spirits.

Ritual: Saining for the Home

Use this ritual to smoke cleanse the energy in your home.

Needs

Bundle of dried juniper, rowan, and heather, and matches.

Directions

Light a bundle of herbs. Walking clockwise through the home as the smoke rises, focusing on doorways, windows, and corners, say, "By smoke and spirit, this space is cleansed. No harm may enter; only peace remains." Allow the smoke to clear, and visualise the home protected by the sacred herbs' energy.

Ritual: Alternative Cleansing Option

For those who seek an even stronger layer of protection, look to the moon and its ancient connection to water. The waters of the moon, blessed under its glowing light, carry the moon's cleansing and protective energy.

Needs

A small bowl, water, and a clear quartz or an amethyst crystal.

Directions

Take a small bowl of this water and place it near the entrance, knowing it will act as a filter, catching and dissolving any negative energy before it can pass through. To heighten the water's magickal properties, add the quartz to amplify its protective energy or amethyst for spiritual clarity. Every time you refresh the water, whisper, "Waters of the moon, pure and clear, guard this threshold; keep all harm from here."

The moon's power is ever present, and through its waters, your doorway remains attuned to the cycles of protection, constantly renewed and empowered.

BACK DOOR AND WINDOW PROTECTION

While much attention is given to the front door as the guardian of the home, it's essential not to overlook the back door and windows, which are gateways through which energy flows. These portals may be more discreet but are no less significant in maintaining your home's spiritual and energetic integrity. Unprotected, these entry points can allow physical forces and spiritual energies to slip inside unnoticed. In-home protection, fortifying all entrances, ensures that your sanctuary remains guarded on all sides.

Ritual: Back Door Protection

This protection ritual is like the front door ritual. You will also be using a protective token. A mirror, for example, can be used to reflect negative energy to its source. If you prefer dried herbs, be sure to make your bundle before starting the ritual.

Needs

A broom or besom, black salt, a small protective charm such as a small mirror or a bundle of rosemary, and bay leaves bound with red thread.

Directions

As with the front door, begin by energetically cleansing the back door. Sweep away stagnant energy with your besom, envisioning any negativity being drawn out with each stroke, much like sweeping away dust. As you approach the threshold of the back door, you can sprinkle black salt across the doorway for protection. Black salt, known for its protective qualities, absorbs negative energy and seals the space from unwanted spiritual intrusions. As you sprinkle the black salt, speak these words with intent: "By salt and broom, I cleanse this door; no harm shall enter forevermore. By earth and bone, by flame and sea, this back door is sealed, so mote it be."

Next, hang a protective charm above the back door. As you hang the charm, feel the magick flow through your fingers, anchoring the protective energy. Whisper the following: "With this charm, this door is sealed; no force of ill shall be revealed. Spirits kind, I call to thee; guard this door and set it free."

Optional

For those seeking even stronger protection, consider carving or drawing a protection sigil onto the inside of the doorframe. See chapter 11 for ideas. Feel the sigil silently reinforcing the boundary between your inner sanctuary and the world beyond each time you pass through.

Ritual: Window Protection

Windows, like doors, serve as liminal spaces, portals between the outside world and your home's inner sanctuary. These openings can be vulnerable to unwanted energies, especially if they are left unguarded. To prevent negative energies from entering through your windows, you should perform a cleansing ritual that uses dragon's blood resin, which is a powerful protector that acts as a fiery guardian, reinforcing the spiritual boundary of the windows. It will ensure that only positive energy may pass through.

Needs

Dragon's blood resin and moon water or water mixed with sea salt. Optional: bundles of dried rosemary, common sage, or lavender tied with red string.

Directions

Begin by thoroughly cleansing the windows, both physically and energetically. Wipe down the windowpanes with a cloth soaked in moon water or water mixed with sea salt, purifying the space. As you clean, envision the water drawing out any stagnant energy that may have accumulated. As you do this, say, "By water's flow and salt so pure, I cleanse these windows, protection sure."

As you place the resin on the sill, visualise a fiery red shield around the window, preventing any malevolent force from entering your space. Once the windows are cleansed, sprinkle a small amount of dragon's blood powder or resin onto the windowsills while saying, "Blood of the dragon, fierce and bright, guard these windows and seal them tight. By fire's strength and magick's will, let no ill cross this window's sill."

Optional

You can also hang small bundles of protective herbs above or along the windows to act as natural protectors, guarding the space from spiritual and energetic intrusion. As you hang the herbs, say, "By leaf and root, by stem and flower, protect this space with ancient power." Repeat this process for each window in your home, ensuring that no entrance remains unguarded.

CREATING WARDS AND ENERGY SHIELDS

When working with home protection, one of the most effective methods is layering various techniques to form multiple levels of defence. This ensures your home is safeguarded physically, energetically, and spiritually. One of the best ways to do this is through wards and energy shields.

ENERGY SHIELDS

Visualising a protective barrier around your home is an excellent way to set strong boundaries. To create a shield, simply close your eyes and picture a glowing sphere of light forming around your entire home. This light can be any colour that resonates with you: gold for divine protection, blue for Archangel Michael's shield, or white for pure, spiritual light. Envision the light expanding outward, covering your roof, walls, windows, and the land around your home.

Now say, "By the power of the light I weave, no harm may enter, no darkness deceive. This home is sealed, strong and bright, protected by day and throughout the night." Repeat this visualisation daily or weekly to reinforce the shield. Over time, it will grow stronger, becoming a potent barrier that keeps your home safe from harm.

WARDS

Wards are protective objects or symbols placed around your home to create a boundary that blocks unwanted energy or entities. They can be physical items, such as crystals, iron nails, or witch bottles, or energetic symbols like sigils and runes. Place wards strategically throughout your home, near doors, windows, and corners, to form a protective network.

To set wards, simply gather items that represent protection to you, such as black tourmaline, iron, or herbs like rosemary and thyme. Place these items at your chosen points around the home, and as you do, say, "Ward of strength, ward of light, protect this space day and night. No harm may cross this boundary by the old ways and spirits' decree." Refresh wards regularly to incorporate them into your routine, especially during the critical lunar phases of the new or full moon.

THE HEART OF THE HOME

The hearth has traditionally been not just a place where food was once prepared; it was the very soul of the home, the sacred centre where warmth, nourishment, and protection intertwined. The fire that burned within the hearth was more than just physical flame; it was a symbol of the family's spirit, a guiding light that warded off the darkness of the outside world and invited blessings into the heart of the household. It was here, beside the crackling flames, that stories were told, offerings were made, and protection spells were woven into the very fabric of the home.

The hearth's energy connected the living with the divine, bridging the realms of the seen and unseen. The sacred fire was kept burning as a form of constant magickal protection, ensuring the family remained safe, prosperous, and protected from harm. It was believed that the spirits of the ancestors, the hearth guardians, and the very essence of the land found solace in the warmth of the hearth's flame. Allowing the fire to die out risked inviting misfortune, leaving the home vulnerable to malevolent forces.

While many modern homes no longer have a traditional fireplace, the magick of the hearth remains. In today's world, the kitchen often serves as the contemporary hearth, where nourishment is created, and the home's energies are anchored and renewed. The stove, where meals are lovingly prepared, can be viewed as a modern altar of flame. Protecting this sacred space ensures that the home's warmth, love, and protection continue to flow freely.

Ritual: Cleansing and Guarding the Hearth

You will begin your hearth protection with a cleansing ritual. Whether you have a traditional hearth or a kitchen stove, this space holds and radiates energy. Before invoking any protection, it is vital to purify the area to dispel stagnant or negative vibrations. Then you will proceed to protect the space.

Needs

A candle, salt, and a piece of mirror or a piece of iron (e.g., a nail, trinket, or horseshoe).

Directions

Light a candle, a symbol of both the ancient hearth fire and the element of spirit. As the flame flickers, visualise its light expanding throughout the hearth or kitchen, burning away any lingering negativity or stagnant energy. The candle's flame acts as a purifier, consuming the old to make way for the new. Speak this charm as you hold your intention steady: "By salt and flame, I guard this hearth. No ill shall dwell, no harm take part."

As the flame dances, you may also choose to sprinkle salt around the perimeter of the hearth or stove. As an ancient protector, salt creates an energetic boundary that ensures no ill-willed energy may settle in this sacred space. Feel the salt's protective energy merging with the flame's purifying force.

To further guard the hearth, place a piece of mirror near it or on the mantle to reflect negative energy. Or place a simple iron nail, trinket, or horseshoe, which can serve as a powerful anchor for protective energies. Iron has long been revered in folk magick for its ability to ward off malevolent spirits and shield against harmful energy. As you set the iron in place, visualise it, solidifying the hearth's defences. Speak these words of power: "Iron strong, protect this space; guard this hearth with steadfast grace."

Optional

If your home lacks a traditional hearth, consider creating a small altar in the kitchen or dining area. This altar can serve as a hearth space, a sacred spot where the energy of fire is represented through candles, stones, and symbols of protection. Place items that resonate with the fire element, such as candles, red or gold stones, or protective crystals like black tourmaline on the altar. This altar will become the heart of your home, offering protection and warmth to all who enter.

KEEPING THE HEARTH FLAME ALIVE

The hearth is a living entity, constantly shifting and evolving in response to the home's energy. To maintain its protective force, it is essential to keep its energy strong and vibrant. One of the simplest yet most powerful ways is to regularly light a candle at the centre of the hearth or kitchen. Whether during daily rituals or when the air feels heavy with worry, this small flame can invoke the protective energy of the sacred hearth fire.

Each time you light the candle, allow its flame to connect with the ancient fires that have burned in hearths. Feel its warmth spreading through your home, filling every room with safety and protection. As you gaze into the flame, whisper, "Flame of hearth, burn bright and strong; keep us safe where we belong." Let the flame remind you that your home is a sanctuary and that you, as the keeper of the hearth, wield the power to protect those who dwell within its walls.

HERBAL MAGICK FOR THE HEARTH

Just as herbs are used to flavour and nourish the food that sustains us, they also possess powerful magickal properties that can be woven into hearth protection rituals. Cooking itself is an alchemical process, and the herbs you choose can carry protective and healing energies that benefit not only the body but also the spirit. Burn rosemary, bay leaves, or cinnamon sticks in the hearth to create a potent barrier against negativity. These herbs are known for their protective properties and have been used in magickal practices to ward off harm and invite blessings. As the smoke rises, see it forming a protective shield around your home, sealing it from unwanted energies.

HEARTH SPIRITS AND OFFERINGS

In many magickal traditions, the hearth is considered a sacred dwelling for guardian spirits. These hearth spirits watch over the home and its inhabitants, offering protection and guidance to those who honour them. They are ancient beings, deeply connected to the land and the ancestors who came before, and their presence within the hearth flame acts as a guardian force that shields the family from harm.

You can honour the spirits of the hearth by making small offerings as a token of gratitude. Herbs, honey, and bread are traditional offerings that can be left near the hearth or stove. Set aside time to connect with these spirits once a month, preferably during the new or full moon. Prepare a small dish with your chosen offering and place it at the hearth's centre. As you do so, speak words of gratitude: "Spirits of hearth, I honour thee; protect this home and all who be. By flame and smoke, by hearth's warm light, guard our space day and night." This simple yet profound act strengthens your bond with the hearth spirits, inviting them to continue watching over your home and offering their protective guidance.

As with any magickal relationship, regularly renewing your offerings to the hearth spirits is essential. Each new or full moon refreshes the offerings, cleansing the area and adding new tokens of appreciation. Doing so nurtures a reciprocal relationship, ensuring that the hearth spirits remain strong and vigilant in protecting your home.

The hearth remains the magickal and spiritual centre of the home, even in modern times. Whether you have a roaring fireplace, a simple stove, or an altar dedicated to the fire element, the energy of the hearth continues to offer protection, warmth, and safety. By tending to your hearth with intention and reverence, you weave powerful magick into the heart of your home, creating a sanctuary that nurtures, protects, and empowers all who enter.

Ritual: Protection Against Electrical and Radiation Stress

Many homes are situated near electricity pylons, telephone masts, or other sources of electromagnetic radiation. These forces can disrupt the energy field of your home, creating a constant background disturbance that affects both your physical and energetic well-being. We can create energetic shields and use protective materials to minimise the impact of these modern stresses.

Needs

A black tourmaline stone (for grounding and absorbing harmful energy), aluminium foil (to reflect radiation), and a small mirror (to reflect energy).

Directions

Begin by placing a black tourmaline near the areas of your home where electrical devices are most concentrated, such as near your Wi-Fi router, television, or power outlets. Black tourmaline is known for absorbing and neutralising harmful electromagnetic fields, acting as a shield for your space. Next, place a small mirror in the area where you feel the most geopathic stress or electromagnetic influence. The mirror will reflect and deflect the energy away from your home, ensuring it does not accumulate or affect you.

To further enhance protection, you can line certain surfaces with aluminium foil, especially near windows or walls facing electricity pylons or telephone masts. The foil is a barrier, reflecting harmful electromagnetic waves away from your home. As you set these protections in place, say, "By tourmaline's might and mirror's gleam, protect this space, my sacred dream. No stress may enter, no harm may flow, and by my will, protection grows."

13
ENERGY OF FORGOTTEN PLACES

Beneath the concrete and stone of modern structures lies the ancient pulse of the earth, lands that have witnessed battles, burials, and centuries of history. When businesses or homes are constructed on old battlefields, cemeteries, or sacred ground, the energy of the past doesn't simply disappear. It remains woven into the earth, often unnoticed by those who build above it but deeply felt by those sensitive to the unseen currents of the land.

RESIDUAL ENERGY

Spirits and energies tied to the land can become restless, significantly, when modern construction disturbs the sanctity of a battlefield or burial site. It is our responsibility and gift to protect, cleanse, and harmonise our spaces, ensuring peace and balance for ourselves and the land beneath our feet. It is also essential to recognise the signs of lingering energies in old buildings that you may not work in. Whether you work in an old hospital, a factory building, or a new building constructed on a former battlefield, cemetery, or ancient sacred site, the land and space may carry the imprints of trauma, death, or unresolved issues.

These imprints can manifest in you and your coworkers as uneasy feelings or cold spots in certain rooms, recurring nightmares or feelings of being watched, disturbances such as objects moving or strange noises, or heavy, stagnant energy that never seems to clear. The land or building may call for attention, protection, and healing if you sense these signs. Using magickal techniques and rituals, you can protect your home and the lands and buildings beyond from the unseen forces, ensuring that the energy within your space remains balanced, peaceful, and harmonious.

Following are three workings to help you protect and cleanse the space around you.

Ritual: Cleansing and Blessing Old Buildings

Before beginning, it is very important to ask the spirits of the house and the land for permission to live and work in the building and outside areas connected to this property. When you inhabit or work in a building constructed on energetically charged land, performing a thorough cleansing and blessing of the space is crucial.

This ritual will clear any lingering energies and honour the spirits tied to the land, bringing peace and harmony to your space.

Needs

A white candle (for purity and peace), a bundle of mugwort, rosemary or juniper (for cleansing), and a bowl of salt water or moon water (for purification).

Directions

Begin by lighting the white candle, inviting peace and light into the space. As the flame burns, walk through each room, gently waving the bundle of herbs to allow the cleansing smoke to fill the air. As you walk, chant, "By earth and flame, by water and air, I cleanse this space with magick fair. Let all who dwelled here find their peace; by my will, all unrest cease."

After you've cleansed each room, sprinkle the salt water or moon water around the perimeter of the building, creating a protective barrier that will keep unwanted energies from returning.

Ritual: Blessing the Land Beneath

Often it's not just the building that needs protection but the land itself. To honour the spirits of the land, whether soldiers, ancestors, or forgotten souls, perform a simple blessing outside the building.

Needs

Milk, honey, or mead.

Directions

Begin by standing barefoot on the ground, feeling the earth beneath you. Pour a small offering of milk, honey, or mead into the earth, symbolising your respect for the spirits and your intent to live in harmony with the land. As you pour, say, "Spirits of land and spirits of old, I offer my peace, heart, and soul. Rest now in peace, in harmony dwells; earth's sacred spell protects this land."

Leave the offering, knowing you have honoured those who came before, and seal the space with protection and goodwill.

Spell: Barrier Spell for Battlefield or Cemetery Energy

Buildings constructed on battlefields or ancient cemeteries can carry the weight of unresolved trauma. In these cases, cleansing the space is not enough; you must create a barrier between your workplace and the land beneath it, ensuring that the energy of past conflict or burial does not seep into your space.

Needs

Four black tourmaline stones, a small mirror, and a red thread.

Directions

Place one black tourmaline stone at each corner of your home to create an energetic grid that shields the building from harmful energy. As you place each stone, say, "Stone of earth, strong and true, protects this home from all that's due." By the power of land and by the sea, I seal this space, so may it be." Next, take the small mirror and wrap it in the red thread. Place the mirror near the entrance of the home, facing outward. This will return any negative energy to its source, ensuring it does not enter your space. Speak this charm as you place the mirror: "Mirror bright, reflect with might; no harm shall enter, no wrong shall stay. By my will, it's sealed this day."

GEOPATHIC STRESS

In modern times, many homes are built over areas of geopathic stress, lines of disturbed energy caused by underground water, electricity pylons, or telephone masts. This disturbed energy can cause unrest in the home, leading to physical and emotional discomfort.

Symptoms of geopathic stress include insomnia, anxiety, headaches, and an overall feeling of unease in some regions of the home. As wise individuals, we can harness the earth's energy to neutralise geopathic stress and create a sanctuary of peace within our homes.

RECOGNISING THE SIGNS OF GEOPATHIC STRESS

Before working to neutralise geopathic stress, it's essential to recognise the signs that your home or workplace may be affected. These signs may include:

- Difficulty sleeping, particularly in certain rooms.
- Unexplained health issues, such as headaches, anxiety, or fatigue.
- Feelings of unease or tension in specific areas of your home.
- Plants are struggling to grow, and pets are avoiding particular spaces.
- Electrical issues or frequent technological malfunctions in specific areas.

If you've noticed any of these symptoms, geopathic stress may be affecting your home or workplace. Below are three workings to help you with geopathic stress.

Ritual: Geopathic Stress Cleansing

This ritual will ensure that your home remains a sanctuary, even if it is built on energetically charged land or affected by geopathic stress. By honouring the spirits and energies tied to the earth, you create harmony between the past and present, ensuring peace for you and the land.

Needs

A clear quartz crystal (for amplification), a bowl of salt water or moon water, and an iron nail or piece of iron (for grounding the energy).

Directions

Walk through your home with the clear quartz crystal, visualising it absorbing any geopathic stress or disturbed energy. As you move through each room, chant,

"Crystal bright, absorb and clear, all stress and harm, no longer here. By earth and stone, I cleanse this space and fill it with peace, love, and grace."

Once you have completed the cleansing, place the iron nail in the ground outside the main entrance of the home. This will act as a grounding anchor, neutralising the geopathic stress and preventing it from affecting your home. As you bury the iron, say, "This home is grounded, safe and bright by iron's strength and earth's pure might. No stress may enter, no harm shall stay, by my will, it's done this day."

Ritual: Harmonising the Earth and Water Energies

One of the most common causes of geopathic stress is the presence of underground water veins or rivers that flow beneath the house, disrupting the natural energy flow. These hidden waters can cause an imbalance between the earth and water elements, leading to energetic disturbances that affect the home's overall harmony. You can restore balance and protect your space by working with the elements.

Needs

A bowl of earth or salt (to represent the earth element), a small bowl of blue water (unfiltered—not tap water—to represent the water element), and a green candle (for balance and harmony).

Directions

Begin by placing the bowls of earth and water on a central altar or near the area of your home that is affected. Light the green candle, calling upon the forces of nature to help you restore balance between the elements. As the candle burns, place your hands over the bowl of earth and say, "By the strength of the earth, solid and true, I call upon you to ground this space, to bring stability and protection beneath my feet."

Next, place your hands over the bowl of water and say, "By the flow of the water, pure and bright, I call upon you to harmonise and cleanse, to bring peace and balance to this place."

Finally, hold the green candle in your hands and visualise the energies of the earth and water weaving together in harmony, balancing the forces beneath your home. As you do this, say, "By earth and water, strong and free, the balance now returns to me. No stress may stay, no harm may flow, only peace and light may grow. So, mote it be." Allow the candle to burn for a while, visualising the energy of balance spreading through your home and neutralising any geopathic stress caused by water veins or earth imbalances.

Spell: The Iron Nail Technique

Iron is an excellent grounding material for areas affected by geopathic stress, especially those with underground water veins or fault lines. The ancient technique of placing an iron nail in the ground can help anchor and neutralise these energies, protecting your home.

Needs

A large iron nail or iron rod, a hammer, and a bowl of salt water (for purification).

Directions

Begin by dipping the iron nail into the bowl of salt water, purifying and charging it with the intention of grounding and protecting your space. As you do this, say, "Iron strong, by earth and sea, protect this home, so mote it be." Once the nail has been charged, go outside and find a suitable place to drive it into the ground, ideally near the area where you feel the most geopathic stress.

Hammer the nail into the earth, visualise it, anchor the disruptive energy, and return it to the earth, where it can be neutralised.

As you drive the nail into the ground, say, "Iron's strength and earth's deep core, protect this space forever. No stress may arise, and no harm may stay; this home is safe, both night and day." The iron nail will act as a constant anchor, grounding the geopathic stress and preventing it from affecting your home or energy.

DRAWING BOUNDARIES WITH WEE

Swein Macdonald, known as the Highland Seer, had a way of teaching that made every lesson feel as if it were born from the very land itself. He believed that protection wasn't just about casting grand spells but about tapping into our most primal instincts and the natural boundaries we carry within us, just like animals who fiercely protect their territory.

One day, while walking along the edge of the forest above his croft, he stopped and turned to me with that knowing gleam in his eyes. "You have to understand your wee!" he said. I was initially confused, unsure of what he meant. He saw my hesitation and smiled with his big grin. "Your wee is your personal essence, your scent. Every creature in nature has it, and they use it to define their space, to say, 'This is mine; do not cross.'" He explained I could create boundaries around my home using my wee much like an animal marks its territory. This was something deeply personal, an offering of myself to protect the spaces that meant the most to me.

Swein also taught me that the foods I ate before performing this ritual could further strengthen the protection. "Garlic," he said, "is as ancient as the hills and known for its fierce ability to ward off evil. Eat it, and it will enhance your personal power." He suggested I eat garlic, onions, and fiery herbs like rosemary and basil, which are full of protective energy. These foods, imbued with nature's own defences, would make my wee even more potent. All I would then need to do is collect my wee and walk the boundary of my home and garden, pouring the mixture of my wee deliberately around the boundaries.

Swein's teachings went beyond simple spells; they connected me to the earth, to my own body, and to the ancient magick that flows through all things. Every time I perform that ritual, walking the boundary of my home or other space, I feel that connection again. My space, my protection, my boundaries are mine, and nothing unwanted shall cross them. Give this simple technique a try.

14
SHIELDING OUT IN THE WORLD

There was a time when I worked for the airlines, a job I loved dearly. The freedom of the skies, the joy of serving passengers, and the thrill of travel were a dream. But within that dream was a shadow that darkened my days and left me feeling stripped of my power. My boss, the one who should have been a guide and mentor, became my tormentor.

In the middle of the cabin, surrounded by passengers, she would scold me, belittling me with venomous words in front of all who watched. The looks of concern on the passengers' faces were unmistakable, yet their empathy did little to shield me from the constant onslaught. It wasn't just a matter of harsh words; it was a calculated stripping away of my dignity and confidence day by day. And yet, I needed that job. I loved that job. So, I endured, holding on to whatever threads of power I could find.

This experience taught me the importance of protecting oneself every day while traveling, conducting business and otherwise moving about in the mundane world. This is especially true where power dynamics can be manipulated and exploited.

I carry this lesson with me to this day, and I now offer it to you. Whether in the physical workplace, traveling, or online, you deserve to feel safe and empowered, no matter where you work or how you interact with the world. Through magickal protection, we will weave a shield around you, helping you stand tall in the face of adversity. Together, we will reclaim the power others have tried to steal and create a sanctuary for your spirit amid chaos.

PROTECTION MAGICK IN THE WORKPLACE

You are stepping into a complex web of energies when you enter the workplace, whether it's a corporate office, a service role, or even a remote digital space. Some are positive, flowing in harmony with your own, but others can be draining, manipulative, or harmful. These energies, much like the toxic behaviour I endured, can slowly chip away at your spirit, leaving you feeling small, powerless, and trapped. But as witches and magickal beings, we are never truly powerless.

Magick is not only for the sacred circles or full moon rituals; it is woven into every aspect of your life. Your power does not diminish when you walk through your workplace doors or log into your virtual meeting. It is here, in these spaces, where magick is often needed most. Whether you're facing a demanding boss, toxic coworkers, or the sharp sting of a passive-aggressive email, there are countless ways to protect your energy and stand in your power.

YOUR ENERGETIC WORK SHIELD

Before stepping into the workplace, take a moment to ground yourself and create an energetic shield around your body. This ward will act as an invisible barrier, deflecting negative energies and preventing the harsh words or hostile behaviour of others from penetrating your energy field.

Wards are the silent sentinels of magick, woven with intention and anchored by ancient forces. They create an unseen barrier between you and the world's shadows, protecting against harm, ill will, and unwanted energy. Whether placed upon your home, workspace, or digital realm, they stand firm, deflecting negativity and shielding your sacred space.

Spell: How to Create a Simple Personal Shield

To craft a ward is to summon the elements, spirits, and your power, sealing them together in an unbreakable bond of protection. With each ward cast, you claim your space, declaring it inviolable and safe.

Needs

A quiet space.

Directions

Sit or stand in a quiet space before leaving for work. Close your eyes and take three deep breaths. Visualise a glowing, protective light surrounding you; it could be silver, gold, or a colour that resonates with your intention. See this light expanding and solidifying into a shield, strong yet flexible, allowing only positivity to flow through.

Now speak aloud or in your mind, "By the light of my power and the strength of my will, I shield myself from all ill. No harm may touch me; no malice may pass.

I stand protected in a magickal cast. So mote it be." Carry this shield with you throughout the day, knowing that it will deflect the negative energy of coworkers and bosses, as well as the passive aggression conveyed through emails or online messages.

WARDING YOUR WORKSPACE

Your desk or workspace is an extension of your energy. It is where you spend significant time, so it must be guarded and cleaned regularly. The energies of stress, envy, and competition can accumulate in this space, making it vital to ward your workspace as you would a sacred altar. Place black tourmaline, obsidian, or hematite around your desk.

You can whisper a blessing as you place them: "Stones of the earth, guardians of light, protect this space from all blight. No harm may enter, no ill may stay; I work in peace, by night and day." These stones will absorb and deflect negativity, acting as sentinels to guard your energy throughout the day.

You can also carry a piece of clear quartz or labradorite to enhance your power and clarity or sage spray in your bag or pocket. If you encounter any problems, take a break and spray your aura. Discreetly tuck a sachet of protective herbs, such as rosemary or bay leaves, into a drawer or under your keyboard. These herbs have powerful protective properties that shield your workspace from unwanted energies. As you place them, say, "By leaf and root, I seal this space; no harm may enter this sacred place."

WARDING OFF NEGATIVE ENERGY FROM COWORKERS

The workplace can sometimes feel like a battlefield of energy. People carry their personal frustrations, jealousies, and negative emotions into the workspace, often unknowingly affecting those around them. Even with a strong shield, specific individuals may still try to push their negative energy into your space. This is where warding becomes essential.

Spell: Create a Warding Sigil

Sigils are powerful symbols charged with intention. They can be discreetly drawn onto objects in your workspace or worn as jewellery to provide constant protection.

Needs

Paper and pen.

Directions

Take a piece of paper and write down "I am protected from all negativity." Remove the vowels and any repeating letters until you have a few letters. Arrange these letters into a symbol or pattern that feels protective to you.

Once the sigil is created, charge it by holding it and focusing on it. Visualise the sigil glowing with protective energy. Now draw this sigil on a small object on your desk, perhaps on a piece of paper tucked into a drawer or even traced with your finger on your phone or computer. Each time you see or think of the sigil, remember it actively removes the negative energies around you.

DEALING WITH BULLIES AND TOXIC COWORKERS

When faced with a toxic boss or a bullying coworker, it can feel as though your power is being stripped from you with every encounter. But you are not without defence. Words of power, spoken with intent, can change the energy of any situation, transforming the dynamic and allowing you to reclaim your strength.

When someone begins to berate or belittle you, take a deep breath and repeat in your head, "I stand in my power, untouched and whole. Your words cannot harm me, nor touch my soul." Now visualise their words bouncing off your shield, unable to penetrate or cause harm. Excuse yourself from the situation if necessary, knowing that their energy has no hold over you.

DEFENDING YOUR ENERGY IN THE DIGITAL REALM

In the ever-expanding digital world, the screen may seem like a barrier, but energy moves as swiftly online as in person. Words carry power, and those who seek to hurt, bully, or troll others through the safety of their screens can leave energetic wounds if left unchecked.

Online bullying—whether through social media, emails, or other digital spaces—can feel just as draining and damaging as being attacked face-to-face. However, just as we ward our physical spaces, we can weave powerful protection spells and shields to defend our online presence and turn the negative energy of trolls back to its source.

SHIELDING YOUR ONLINE PRESENCE

Every time you engage in the digital realm—whether through work emails, social media, or online forums—imagine that your energetic field extends into this virtual space. It would help to protect your energy here as in any physical space. Here's how to craft a shield specifically for your digital interactions.

Before logging on, take a moment to ground and centre. Close your eyes and visualise a light shield surrounding your online presence, post, message, and interaction. This shield can be golden for protection, blue for peace, or silver to reflect negative energy away. Speak this incantation: "By light and code, my space is clear; no ill shall reach me, and none shall come near. My words are guarded, my energy safe; no harm shall find me in this place." This shield will stay with you throughout your digital interactions, repelling negativity and preventing it from attaching to you.

TECH TALISMANS

Create a talisman specifically for your online protection. This could be a small charm or crystal or a sigil drawn onto paper. Keep it near your computer or in your bag while working online, allowing its protective energy to create a buffer between you and the digital world.

A simple charm could be a small piece of clear quartz for clarity and protection or hematite for grounding. Hold the stone in your hand and charge it with your intention by saying, "By this charm, I stand shielded. No malice shall touch me; no harm shall find me. My online space is protected; by my will, it is done."

Even with protection, bullying can happen. The next spell will help.

Spell: Online Bullying Banishing

When you encounter online bullying, standing in your power and refusing to absorb the harmful energy is essential. This spell allows you to banish the bullying energy and return it to its source, ensuring it does not take root in your life.

Needs

A piece of paper, a pen (but if you have a quill and ink, even better), and a small jar or bowl of salt.

Directions

Write the name or handle of the troll or bully on the piece of paper. If the person is anonymous or you don't know their name, you can write, "The energy of online harm." Fold the paper away from you three times, saying, "Energy of harm, I banish thee; no longer shall you have power over me. What you send returns to you, by my will, so mote it be true." Place the folded paper in the jar or bowl of salt and seal it with the words, "Salt's power and ancient decree neutralise this harm; you cannot harm me." The salt absorbs and neutralises the energy. Once the situation feels resolved, dispose of the salt outside, knowing that the bullying energy has been banished.

CLEANSING AFTER ONLINE ATTACKS

Some residual energy may linger in your space even after deflecting online negativity. It's essential to cleanse your energy field and digital devices regularly to ensure that no traces of negativity remain. Use smoke from protective herbs such as cedar, mugwort, and juniper or ring a bell near your computer or phone. The sound or smoke will cleanse the device's energy, removing any negativity that may have been attached during your online interactions.

As you cleanse, say, "By smoke (or sound) and pure power, I cleanse this space, and all endure. No harm shall linger, no ill remain, only peace and light sustain." This ritual can be done as often as needed, especially after a particularly negative online interaction.

Ritual: Empowerment in the Digital Space

After dealing with an online attack, reclaiming your energy and power is essential, ensuring that the negative interaction doesn't leave a lasting impact on your well-being. This ritual helps you regain control over your digital space and restore your confidence. You will need to choose a symbol or sigil of protection. It can be one you create or a common one. See chapter 11.

Needs

An orange candle, paper, and a pen.

Directions

Light a red or orange candle, colours associated with confidence, strength, and personal power.

On a piece of paper, draw a sigil that represents reclaiming your digital space. It can be as simple as a symbol of protection or a unique design you create. Hold the sigil in your hands and visualise yourself standing strong, untouched by the negativity.

Feel your energy returning to you, glowing brighter with every breath, and now say, "By flame's light and sigil's might, I reclaim my space and power. No harm shall touch me, no ill shall hold, I stand protected, fierce and bold." Keep the sigil near your computer or phone as a reminder of your magick.

RECLAIMING YOUR POWER

Sometimes, even with all your magickal protections in place, a toxic environment or a vicious online attack can leave a mark on your energy. When this happens, it's time to perform a banishing ritual to release harmful energies and reclaim your power fully.

Ritual: Banishing Toxic Energy

This ritual can be done at home or in a private space at work where you can focus without distractions.

Needs

A red candle, a small bowl of dragon's blood water, and a pinch of red salt.

Directions

Begin by lighting the red candle, a symbol of banishing and protection. Sit quietly for a moment, acknowledging the toxic energy you wish to release, whether it's the memory of a harsh word, a toxic interaction, or the lingering effects of a stressful day.

Now add the salt to the water, stirring it clockwise as you chant, "By salt and dragon's blood water, I cleanse and release. All harm, all hurt, now may cease." Next, gently sprinkle the bowl of water around your workspace or body, visualising the negativity being washed away. As you do, speak these words: "By earth and water, by fire and air, I release this harm into the care of the elements. No longer shall it touch me, for I stand free." Once the candle has burned down, dispose of the water outside or down the drain, carrying the intention that the toxic energy is gone for good.

TRAVEL PROTECTIONS

Just as you weave protection magick into your workplace and online presence, extending that protection into the spaces where you travel is vital. Whether driving in your car, taking the bus, or journeying by air, the energy around you constantly shifts. On the road, you encounter physical dangers and the subtle energies of others moving through the world, some carrying stress, anxiety, or negativity that can linger and affect you if left unchecked.

CAR PROTECTION

Your car is an extension of your energy, a vessel that carries you through the world. Just as you protect and bless your home or workspace, your car can ensure smooth, safe journeys free from accidents or negative influences.

Charm: Protection for the Car

Create a small charm to hang in your car for ongoing protection. You will need a few simple items: a piece of red thread (for protection), a small black obsidian stone (for grounding and shielding), and a sprig of rosemary or lavender (for cleansing).

Tie the stone and herb with the red thread, focusing your intent on the charm's power to protect you on all your travels. As you create the charm, say, "By earth, flame, air, and sea, protect this car and safeguard me. My journey is blessed by fate on every road, through every gate. So mote it be." Now hang the charm from your rearview mirror or tuck it into a safe place in your car, knowing it will act as a guardian during every journey.

Spell: Roadside Warding

Before setting out on a long journey, take a moment to create a ward around your car. Stand beside the vehicle and sprinkle a small line of salt or blessed water around its perimeter, forming a protective circle. As you do, visualise a shield of light surrounding the car, protecting you from accidents, road rage, and other negative energies on the road.

Now, say, "By the road and by the wheel, this car is protected, sealed, and healed. No harm shall find me; no ill shall stay; my path is clear, come night or day." Feel the energy of protection sealing the car in a bubble of light as you embark on your journey.

BUS AND PUBLIC TRANSPORT

Public transport can be a chaotic mix of energies. The proximity to strangers, the stress of commuting, and the general rush of travel can easily overwhelm your energy field. Protecting yourself while riding the bus, train, or subway is essential to ensure you remain grounded and unaffected by the energy around you.

Spell: Energetic Cloak for Public Spaces

Before stepping onto public transport, visualise yourself wrapping an invisible cloak around your body, shielding your energy from others. This cloak will act as a barrier, allowing you to move through crowded spaces without absorbing the power of those around you.

As you mentally put on this cloak, say, "Cloak of shadow, cloak of light, protect my spirit, keep me tight. No harm may touch, no ill shall stay; my energy is mine throughout the day." Imagine the cloak forming a soft, protective layer around you, keeping you centred and grounded no matter how hectic the environment.

Charm for Public Transport

Carry a small charm or stone in your bag or pocket for protection during travel. A piece of black obsidian or hematite can work wonders for absorbing negative energy and keeping you grounded in public spaces.

Charge the stone with your intention before leaving home by holding it in your hands and saying, "Stone of strength, stone of power, protect me in this crowded hour. Absorb all harm, deflect all ill, I remain grounded by my will." Carry the stone with you as a portable shield, allowing its energy to create a barrier between you and the energies around you.

AIR TRAVEL PROTECTION

Air travel carries its unique energies, with so many people passing through the liminal space of airports and planes. Long flights and the bustling energy of terminals can leave you drained or unsettled if you don't protect yourself adequately. Here's how to ensure safe, magickal air journeys.

Spell: Airplane Protection

Before boarding your flight, take a quiet moment to centre yourself. Visualise a protective bubble forming around you and the plane, holding you safely as you journey through the sky. You can place your hands on your seatbelt or have a small charm, like a piece of amethyst or jet, while you cast this spell: "This plane is safe and protected by name, sky, wind, flight, and flame. No harm may come, no fear may rise, and we soar protected through the skies. So mote it be." Imagine the bubble of protection surrounding you, carrying you safely to your destination.

CLEANSING UPON LANDING

After disembarking, especially from long flights, it's essential to cleanse your energy of the residual energies picked up during travel. Once in a private space, wash your hands with water mixed with a few drops of rosemary or lavender oil to clear any energetic debris. As you wash, say, "By water's flow, I cleanse and release. All energy, not mine, returns to peace." This will help restore your energy and bring you back to the centre after a journey through the crowded, often stressful air travel space.

HOTEL SANCTUARIES

When you step into a hotel room, you're walking into a space holding countless energies before you—travellers from every corner of the world, strangers who share the same bed and air. You don't know what energies linger, so cleaning and protecting are essential. I always carry my sage mist or dragon's blood spray, and the moment I enter, I mist the room. Sage and other herb bundles can't be burned due to smoke alarms, but sprays are powerful alternatives. Let your energy be the strongest force in the room. And remember, if the room feels off, you can ask for a different one. It's your space for the night, and your energy must feel at ease. Most hotel windows are sealed, and the air is processed through air conditioning, shutting out fresh elements like air, fire, and earth.

CLEARING THE DAY'S ENERGY

At the end of each day, whether it's after work or travel, it's important to cleanse yourself of the energies you've encountered. Even with strong protection, some negativity may cling to your aura, affecting your mood or draining your energy. A simple end-of-day cleansing ritual will help you release residual energy and restore power.

When you arrive home (or leave your home office), light a white candle and sprinkle a pinch of sea salt into a water bowl.

Dip your fingers into the water and gently flick it around your body, visualising the water absorbing any lingering negativity. Speak these words: "By water and salt, I cleanse and release. All that is heavy, I now release. I am whole and free; by this spell, I am restored to me." Allow the candle to burn for a while as you relax, feeling your energy return to its natural, balanced state.

15
SHIELDING FOR HIGHLY SENSITIVE PEOPLE

As a medium with dyslexia and ADHD, I've come to understand just how essential protection magick is for those of us who are highly sensitive to the world around us. We navigate through layers that others can't see, emotional vibrations, psychic impressions, and the constant energy swirling between the living and spirit realms. This heightened sensitivity is a gift but can also be overwhelming, especially when you're always open and exposed to these unseen forces. Without magickal protection, it's like walking through a storm without shelter, feeling everything at once.

I'm naturally open to receiving messages from the spirit world, but this openness needs to be managed. Without protective barriers, I can quickly become a magnet for energies or entities I haven't invited. Spirits can sense this openness, particularly those who are restless or searching for a means of communication. Protection magick creates the necessary boundaries, allowing us to choose when and with whom to engage rather than being bombarded by any passing energy.

Living with dyslexia and ADHD adds another layer of complexity. My mind processes information in a way that sometimes feels scattered, chaotic, or overstimulated. The constant flow of external energy, emotions, and vibrations can heighten that chaos, leaving me drained or unfocused. Protection magick becomes a filter that helps me manage these energies, preventing emotional overload or psychic burnout.

When I don't set these protective boundaries, I notice my energy becomes scattered, my focus wavers, and I'm more susceptible to anxiety or emotional overwhelm. The magick I weave through spells, wards, and sacred symbols forms a shield that grounds and centres me, allowing me to move through life with clarity and intention. It helps me protect my energy from being absorbed into the chaotic energy of others, whether they're people around me or entities from the unseen world.

For those of us who are highly sensitive, whether mediums, empaths, neurodiverse individuals, or those dealing with mental health challenges such as PTSD, protection magick isn't just helpful—it's necessary. It keeps our energy intact, shields us from harm, and empowers us to use our gifts without being overwhelmed. Though it is not intended to replace conventional medical practices completely, magick becomes the anchor, the boundary, and the shield that allows us to embrace our sensitivities while keeping the storm of external forces at bay.

MANAGING YOUR SENSITIVITIES

By weaving protection into our daily practice, we ensure that our psychic and emotional boundaries remain firm, allowing us to harness the power of our sensitivities without letting them consume us.

Highly sensitive people (HSPs) experience the world with heightened senses; sounds are louder, lights are brighter, and every interaction feels more intense. These sensory floods can overwhelm them, fragile and energetically exposed without protection. Protection magick becomes their ally, a cloak to soften the harsh edges of the world. By invoking the element of water in ritual, HSPs can create a fluid barrier—a veil that allows them to move through the world untouched by the intensity around them. Amulets of protection, such as pendants anointed with lavender oil, create a calming field that deflects chaos. Sigils carved onto the soles of shoes can make a quiet path where the world softens underfoot.

EMPATHS

Spiritually empathetic individuals are natural energy sponges, absorbing the emotions and energies of others like a thirsty earth that drinks rain. While a gift, this sensitivity can often overwhelm, leaving empaths drained and vulnerable to emotional attacks. For an empath, protection magick is not just a tool; it is a necessity, a woven shield against the tides of emotional waves.

Empaths can protect their emotional bodies by creating personal wards, such as drawing protective sigils on their skin or crafting herbal charms. Black tourmaline, worn close to the heart, absorbs unwanted energies, while blackthorn salt baths serve as rituals to cleanse the energy they've unconsciously gathered throughout the day.

MEDIUMS

Those who bridge the physical and spirit worlds need protection more than most. Walking between the realms opens them up to light and shadow; without proper safeguards, they can be vulnerable to malevolent energies. Protection magick is their sacred armour, allowing them to commune with spirits while remaining safe from harm.

NEURODIVERSE INDIVIDUALS

For those who are neurodiverse, such as those with ADHD, autism, or other neurological differences, the world can feel like an overstimulating and chaotic place. Protection is needed from external energies to calm the internal storms that sometimes rage within. Protection magick is a grounding force, helping create boundaries in an unpredictable world.

By calling upon earth energy, neurodiverse witches can anchor themselves, using stones like hematite or iron to build a solid foundation. Rituals that involve repetitive, soothing actions, such as knot magick or beadwork, can serve as both protection and meditation, calming the mind while weaving a shield around the spirit. Sacred oils, like sandalwood or patchouli, can be anointed on the wrists to anchor their energy throughout the day.

PEOPLE WITH MENTAL HEALTH CHALLENGES

Those living with mental health challenges, such as anxiety or depression, often find themselves battling unseen forces within, as well as external energies. Protection for these individuals must be gentle and strong, creating a sanctuary within their spirit while warding off the dark clouds that seek to overwhelm them.

Protection magick helps create that inner sanctuary, a space where they can find refuge. Rose quartz, the stone of self-love, can be kept under the pillow to protect against night terrors and encourage restful sleep. Daily rituals, such as lighting a candle in honour of inner peace, can become acts of self-care, where the flame serves as a beacon, calling forth protective spirits to watch over them. Crafting protective spells infused with lavender and chamomile can be carried in charm bags to soothe anxiety and shield the heart from emotional turbulence.

PSYCHICS

Psychics, like mediums, walk the path between worlds, but their focus is often on reading the energetic signatures of people, places, and objects. This gift can make them vulnerable to psychic attacks or energetic burnout. Protection magick is essential to keep their third eye clear, focused, and shielded from unwanted intrusion.

Psychic witches can draw a veil of protection over their third eye by anointing it with moon-charged oils, such as sandalwood or clary sage, before beginning any psychic work. A crystal grid, laid out in a sacred pattern, can serve as a psychic barrier, preventing energetic parasites from attaching. Casting a protective circle, with guardians posted at each of the four corners, will ensure the psychic remains safe as they peer into the unknown.

SHIELDING THE HEALER

Healers and therapists—whether they work with physical, emotional, mental, or spiritual health—are often near intense energies. This makes them more susceptible to absorbing the negative or chaotic emotions, trauma, and energy from their clients. This can lead to burnout, emotional exhaustion, and even physical ailments over time, making personal protection specifically essential for the following:

ENERGY ABSORPTION

Healers and therapists can unknowingly absorb their clients' energy, especially when dealing with deep emotional or psychological wounds. Protection helps create a boundary between their energy and that of their clients, preventing them from becoming overwhelmed or drained.

- *Emotional Overload*—Regularly working with people in pain or distress can cause emotional fatigue. Protection acts as a buffer, allowing healers and therapists to remain compassionate without being emotionally entangled in their clients' struggles.
- *Energetic Drainage*—If healers are not adequately protected, their personal energy levels may become depleted after sessions. This can lead to fatigue and diminish their ability to offer effective healing over time.
- *Psychic Attacks*—In some cases, healers and therapists can encounter individuals with harmful intentions or unconscious projections of anger, jealousy, or fear. These energies can manifest as psychic attacks, making protection vital to maintaining energetic stability.
- *Empathic Sensitivity*—Many healers and therapists are naturally empathic, which means they are even more sensitive to the energies of others. Without protection, their empathy can become overwhelming, leaving them feeling drained or unwell after sessions.

MAINTAINING CLARITY AND OBJECTIVITY

Protective measures help healers and therapists maintain mental and emotional clarity, preventing them from being swayed by their clients' emotions or issues. This allows them to provide more grounded, effective care. Feel the shield solidify, glowing with the strength of those who have come before you. The witch's shield is now active, standing tall around you, reflecting all harm and ill intent. Stand in your sacred space, knowing you are fully protected, grounded, and held within this ancient defence. Please take a moment to sense the shield's energy, knowing it moves with you, guarding your spirit. When you are ready, close your ritual with gratitude, grounding yourself and returning to your daily path, carrying the shield's strength throughout the day.

PROTECTION IN PERSONAL RELATIONSHIPS

Throughout my life, I've encountered all manner of energetic threats, from narcissists and manipulators to dark entities, parasites, and energy-draining vampires. These individuals and forces have crossed my path in many forms, leaving their marks on my spirit and challenging my personal boundaries. Toxic relationships and manipulative influences can sap the strength of even the most resilient of souls, but as a medium and a sensitive person, the effects can run far deeper.

However, while working at the Arthur Finlay College, I faced the densest layers of these energies. In that environment, surrounded by a potent mix of human egos and spiritual energies, I found myself exposed to more than I had ever imagined, both in human form and beyond. It was a place that magnified my sensitivity and tested every form of protection magick I knew.

In this crucible of spiritual work and psychic connection, I learned the hard way how essential magickal boundaries and protection truly are. I emerged from that experience with a deeper understanding of how necessary it is for highly sensitive people, mediums, empaths, and anyone navigating the realms of spirit and energy to shield themselves. Without protection, we are vulnerable to forces and individuals that can drain, manipulate, or even harm us, but with magickal tools, we can stand in our power, fully shielded and untouchable.

PROTECTING AGAINST ENERGETIC PREDATORS

Empaths, HSPs, mediums, and those who walk with a heightened sensitivity to the world's energies face unique challenges. Not only must they navigate their gifts and sensitivities, but they must also be ever vigilant against those who seek to drain or manipulate their energy. Human and nonhuman predators come in many forms and can disrupt their energetic balance if left unchecked. Knowing who or what to avoid and how to shield against them is essential for protecting their spiritual and emotional well-being.

THE CHARMERS WHO DRAIN

Narcissists are perhaps one of the most dangerous types of people for sensitive individuals to be around. With their charm and ability to draw people in, they appear attractive initially, but often leave devastation. Narcissists feed on attention and emotional energy, draining their victims to feed their egos, leaving the empath or sensitive person feeling exhausted, used, and discarded.

For those with heightened sensitivity, it is crucial to maintain energetic boundaries when dealing with narcissists. These individuals can easily tap into the emotions of an empath, using their gifts against them. A protection ritual involving black obsidian or onyx can act as a mirror, reflecting the narcissist's energy back to them without letting it penetrate the sensitive person's emotional field. Creating an energetic barrier by visualising a protective wall of fire or water surrounding your aura can also help prevent these predators from latching on.

ENERGETIC VAMPIRES

Unlike narcissists, energetic vampires may not always be aware of their actions, but the effect is just as harmful. These people leave you feeling drained after every interaction. They are drawn to the light and energy of sensitive individuals, feeding off their vitality. For empaths and HSPs, this can be especially damaging, as they are often too kind to turn away from someone in need, even at their own expense.

Maintaining regular energy-clearing rituals is essential to protecting against energetic vampires. Salt baths infused with protective herbs like rosemary and hyssop (*Hyssopus officinalis*) can cleanse the aura of any lingering energy. Smoky quartz or hematite can be carried to absorb any energy that is not yours, and regular cord-cutting rituals, using a black candle, or a ritual athame can sever the energetic ties these vampires create.

EMOTIONAL MANIPULATORS

Many sensitive individuals find themselves caught in toxic relationships, drawn to people who seem to need healing or saving. These emotional manipulators can be friends, partners, or family members who rely on the sensitive person's compassion to control or drain them. They often play the victim, demanding time, energy, and emotional support without giving anything in return.

The sensitive individual must discern between healthy support and emotional manipulation in these situations. A personal warding spell, cast with protective symbols like Algiz or the pentacle, can help shield against emotional manipulation. Wearing a piece of jewellery enchanted with rose quartz or black tourmaline constantly reminds them of their boundaries, preventing others from crossing into their sacred emotional space.

PSYCHIC PARASITES

Beyond human threats, mediums, psychics, and sensitive individuals must also guard against nonhuman entities—psychic parasites that attach themselves to their aura and feed off their spiritual energy. These entities can enter through portals opened during spiritual work, dream states, or moments of vulnerability.

Psychic parasites may leave the individual feeling lethargic, disoriented, or plagued by intrusive thoughts. To protect against these unseen predators, mediums and psychics should always cast a circle of protection before engaging in spiritual work. Wearing enchanted jewellery, such as an amulet charged with the protective energy of hematite or iron, can act as a shield against these entities. Burning incense, like frankincense or dragon's blood, purifies the space and prevents these entities from taking hold.

Spell: Boundaries Protection

In witchcraft, the art of setting boundaries is just as crucial as any spell. Toxic relationships, harmful environments, and energy vampires can drain a witch's power, leaving them vulnerable to psychic attacks or emotional harm. Setting clear, magickal boundaries ensures that your energy remains your own and no unwanted influence may enter your space.

Needs

A piece of moldavite or tektite.

Directions

Stand in a sacred space with your chosen stone in hand. Hold the stone to your heart and say, "I cast a circle of protection around me; no harm may enter, no ill intent may remain." Visualise a sphere of golden light from the sun surrounding you, strong and impenetrable. Imagine this light repelling any negative influences, whether from people or the unseen. Carry this stone with you to reinforce your protective boundaries throughout the day.

GUARDING YOUR ENERGY FROM TOXIC CONNECTIONS

Navigating relationships can be a beautiful but delicate journey. While relationships can provide love, support, and growth, they can also become a source of energetic drain when toxic dynamics are at play. When we engage in personal relationships with those who might be manipulative, narcissistic, or energetically parasitic, we often find ourselves giving more than we receive, leading to imbalances that can leave us feeling emotionally and energetically depleted.

For those who walk the witch's path, it is essential to recognise when a relationship turns harmful and arm ourselves with protection magick that ensures we are shielded, empowered, and whole. Protecting our energy in relationships is not about closing off or becoming distant, but about maintaining healthy boundaries and ensuring our spiritual, emotional, and mental well-being remains intact.

RECOGNISING TOXIC ENERGIES IN PERSONAL RELATIONSHIPS

Toxic energies in personal relationships often start subtly but can grow over time, creating emotional confusion and energetic disarray. This cannot be easy to pinpoint for the sensitive soul as our natural inclination is to give, heal, and care for others. However, the following signs can indicate when a relationship may be harmful and when protection magick is needed:

- *Constant Emotional Drain*—After spending time with someone, you feel physically or emotionally exhausted, even if the interaction wasn't overtly hostile.
- *Feeling Manipulated*—You notice patterns of control, manipulation, or emotional blackmail, making you feel trapped or powerless.
- *Energetic Cord Attachment*—You feel an unshakable connection to the person, even when apart, as if their emotions or energy linger and weigh on you long after the interaction has ended.
- *Loss of Self-Identity*—In the relationship, you may lose a sense of who you are, prioritising the other person's needs while ignoring your own.
- *Tension and Anxiety*—You feel a constant sense of anxiety or dread around the person, even if the relationship was once harmonious.

- *Negative Cycles*—You notice recurring cycles of conflict, manipulation, or emotional distance, followed by reconciliation that feels forced or superficial.

Once you have recognised the toxic dynamics in a relationship, the next step is to put magickal solid protections that shield your energy and prevent further harm. This protection allows you to maintain clarity and emotional balance while deciding whether to heal the relationship or move forward from it. Below are powerful methods to establish magickal boundaries in relationships.

Ritual: Cord-Cutting to Sever Energetic Ties

Energetic cords form between individuals in close familial, romantic, or platonic relationships. These cords can transmit both positive and negative energy. When the cords become toxic or draining, it's essential to sever them through a cord-cutting ritual.

Needs

A black candle, scissors or a ritual knife, a representation of the person (a photo, a poppet, or their name written on paper), and sage or incense for cleansing.

Directions

Begin by lighting the black candle, symbolising release and protection. Hold the representation of the person or their name in your hands. Visualise the energetic cord that ties you to them; observe whether it is frayed, dark, or feels heavy. Take the scissors or ritual knife and, with focused intent, cut through the air between you and the representation, saying, "By this blade, I sever the ties that bind. No harm shall pass, and no energy drain shall remain. I reclaim my power, my spirit, and my soul. By this magick, I am whole." As you cut, imagine the cord disintegrating, leaving you free and clear. Sage or incense can cleanse the space around you and disperse any lingering negative energy. Allow the candle to burn down completely, sealing the ritual with its flame.

MAINTAINING PROTECTION MAGICK AND BOUNDARIES IN LOVE

It's important to remember that creating magickal boundaries in personal relationships is not about closing off or preventing love. It ensures the energy exchange remains balanced, loving, and mutual. By maintaining these wards, you are protecting yourself and creating the space for healthier, more fulfilling connections to flourish.

With these protections, you can confidently navigate your relationships without fear of energetic depletion or manipulation. Whether it's through cord-cutting, warding, or recognising toxic energy, you can reclaim your personal power and put in place personal protection to cultivate relationships that support your spiritual and emotional growth.

Spell: Reclaim Your Voice

One of the greatest losses in toxic relationships can be your voice, the ability to speak up for yourself, to say no, or to reclaim your power when someone seeks to take it away. But magick can help you find that voice again, strengthening your confidence and empowering you to stand firm. The word *no* is a shield, a sacred boundary drawn with a single breath. It is a protection spell, casting a circle around your energy, guarding your time, and honouring your worth.

When spoken, it roots you in your power, reminding the world that your will is sovereign and untouchable. Say it: NO. Now, say it again and again until it feels really good and empowering. *No* is life-changing and freeing.

Needs

A small orange candle (for courage and strength), a piece of paper, and a pen for this spell.

Directions

Begin by lighting the candle and taking three deep breaths, grounding yourself in your power. On the paper, write down the situations where you feel your voice has been taken, whether from a toxic partner, a family member, or an online interaction. As you write, visualise the energy of those situations flowing onto the page, leaving your body and mind clear. Fold the paper toward you, saying, "With this act, I reclaim my voice, power, and strength. No one shall silence me, for I am the keeper of my destiny." Now burn the paper in the candle's flame, allowing the smoke to carry your intention into the universe. As the paper burns, say, "Fire's flame frees my voice, smoke's ascent and my will is bent." Let the candle burn for a while as you meditate on your power, feeling your voice return to you, stronger and more vibrant than before.

SHADOW WORK: PROTECTING AND HEALING THE SELF

As we near the completion of this chapter, it is essential to address one of the most profound aspects of magickal protection: shadow work. Shadow work is not about defending yourself from outside energies but from the parts of yourself that you have buried, repressed, or denied. The darker parts of your psyche—the fears, insecurities, and traumas—can weaken your magick and personal power if left unchecked.

In essence, shadow work is a form of inner protection. Acknowledging and integrating these aspects of yourself removes their power to influence you unconsciously. When these hidden parts are left to fester, they can manifest as energetic vulnerabilities, attracting negative experiences, relationships, or spiritual attachments.

For HSPs, shadow work is essential because our openness to external energies also makes us vulnerable to the energies within ourselves. If we do not confront our shadows, we leave gaps in our protective barriers, allowing outside forces to exploit our insecurities, doubts, and fears.

By doing shadow work, you actively protect yourself by healing the parts of you that are most susceptible to energetic attacks. This work requires courage, which involves facing the darkest parts of your soul, but it is the key to true empowerment and magickal resilience.

JOURNALING YOUR SHADOWS

Write down the fears, insecurities, or painful memories you avoid facing. As you do, you begin bringing these shadows to light. Once they are visible, they lose much of their power over you.

RITUAL RELEASE

Create a ritual where you symbolically release your shadows. Please write down your fears or unresolved emotions on paper, then burn them in a cauldron or fireproof dish, releasing their hold on you and transforming their energy into strength.

MEDITATION AND SELF-REFLECTION

Through deep meditation, allow your mind to drift to the darker aspects of your psyche. Acknowledge them without judgment, understanding they are part of your personal growth and evolution.

EMBRACING THE SHADOW FAMILIAR

In witchcraft, some practitioners call upon their shadow familiar, a spiritual guide that helps them navigate the dark recesses of their psyche. By befriending this aspect of yourself, you can gain deeper insight into your shadows and turn them into power sources.

We embrace inner protection and shadow work to create a holistic approach to magickal protection. Shielding ourselves from outside energies is not enough; we must also protect ourselves from within, ensuring that our magick is strong, unshakable, and grounded in self-awareness and healing.

16
DREAM PROTECTION

When twilight merges into night and your body surrenders to rest, your spirit stirs as it waits for the sacred threshold to open. It is the eternal realm of creation, where ancestral spirits shaped land, sky, and water through song and story. It is not a memory but a living realm—woven into the earth, the stars, and the blood. One may enter it through dreams, trance, or sacred rite, but always with reverence. It is a place of power where spirit law is upheld, and nothing passes unseen.

When I was in Australia in 2002, I was honoured to go walkabout with the Aboriginal people and undergo rites of initiation into the Dreaming in a cave near the heart of the red earth, not far from Uluru. There, the veil parted, and I glimpsed the pulse of the land—alive with spirit and memory.

Later that year, I continued my journey to South America, deep into the Amazon jungle. There, on sacred land, I was taken on a journey by the curandero—the medicine man—who taught me about the Dreamtime from another path of understanding, guiding me through the dimensions the soul must traverse as it journeys beyond the veil. Through plant spirit, chant, and silence, I walked into realms where shadow and light held court, where the soul was tested, stripped, and shown its truth.

Both journeys were life-changing—ones that opened my eyes to worlds layered within this one. Realms that exist just beyond the edge of waking, where the true magick begins and the hidden aspects of the Dreamtime reveal themselves: the guardians, the gateways, the trials, and the truths waiting to be reclaimed.

Before modern minds dismissed dreams as fantasy, many ancient peoples saw them as gateways to divine and hidden realms—places of power requiring protection. In Egypt, sacred dreaming was part of temple rites, where the ka—the soul-double—journeyed through the Duat, the unseen realm of gods and spirits. Amulets were worn, and prayers were spoken to guard the sleeper from shadowy beings. In ancient Greece, seekers entered incubation chambers within healing temples, where they fasted, invoked the gods, and slept beneath sacred symbols, shielded by ritual to receive prophetic dreams without interference, guarded by those who knew the Dreamtime. Across these ancient worlds, it was known that to dream was to open the soul, and one must never open to the Dreamtime unguarded.

CLEANSING THE BEDROOM

Before any dream spell, ward, or enchantment can truly take hold, the space must first be cleansed—energetically emptied and ritually reset. Like a chalice, the bedroom must be purified before it can hold sacred energy. If old energies linger, your magick may dim or distort, and the spirit may struggle to rest.

Begin by choosing the correct time. Cleansing is best done on a Monday (moon) or Saturday (Saturn). The moon governs dreams, intuition, and psychic flow; Saturn offers boundary, banishment, and stillness. Work during the waning moon to remove negativity or the dark moon for deeper clearing.

Open the windows to allow the energies to shift. Use one or more of the following methods:

- Smoke cleanse with sacred herbs such as mugwort, juniper, or wormwood (*Artemisia absinthium*). Move counterclockwise through the room, beginning at the door, saying, "By smoke and flame, by wind and night, I clear all harm; I claim this rite."
- Anoint the doorways, mirrors, and corners with camphor or lavender oil, drawing a protective sigil or crescent moon at each point. These seal the space from intrusive energies.
- Create a floor wash using moon water, sea salt, and rosemary. Mop or sprinkle it lightly around the bed to cleanse the foundation.
- Sound clear with a bell, singing bowl, or your voice. Sound dislodges psychic residue and creates resonance in the astral layers of the room.

Once the space is cleared, stand at the centre of the room or the foot of your bed. Visualise your bedroom wrapped in a dome of moonlight or obsidian mist. Speak: "This space is sealed by will and flame, no shadow may cross, and no ghost may name. From bed to wall, from floor to sky, only peace and dream shall lie." Proceed to set your dream protections—crystals, herbs, sigils, and wards—knowing the space is now a vessel of sanctuary, ritual, and sacred sleep. Try creating a dream altar.

Spell: The Dream Altar

Craft a sacred altar by your bedside to guide and guard you each night.

Needs

A silver bowl of moon water for scrying or offering; a white or silver candle to echo La Lune light; a sigil, charm, or image of your dream guardian or shadow familiar; and offerings of mugwort, myrrh, camphor, or lavender.

Directions

Build your altar where it can remain in place. Before sleep, light the candle and whisper, "By starlit flame and guardian's grace, I open the veil; I claim my space."

PROTECTION FOR THE DREAM CHAMBER

The bedroom is a portal chamber, a liminal sanctuary where the veil between worlds thins and the soul drifts into other realms. For the witch, seer, or intuitive, the sleep space becomes a ritual site of unconscious magick, where dreams are not random but prophetic, healing, or initiatory. It is during these hours—between waking and deep sleep—when we are most psychically open and spiritually vulnerable.

Without intentional protection, this sacred space may become a ground for stray spirits, thoughtforms, and astral parasites. Residual energies—emotions, projections, even others' dreams—can collect in corners, beneath beds, or in old bedding, influencing your rest and pulling your energy without permission. Just as we would ward our altar or cast a protective circle, we must ward the place where we lay our heads.

SCOTTISH FOLK MAGICK FOR THE SLEEP CHAMBER

Here are some old spells and charms from the Highlands that Swein passed to me to protect the bedroom and the dreamer.

- To shield your bed, hang a Rowan Cross, tied with red thread, above the bed.
- Tuck a small iron blade beneath the mattress to cut through nightmares.
- Suspend a Stone of the Dead, also known as a hagstone (a naturally holed stone) by black thread to repel wandering spirits.
- Lay a line of blackthorn sea salt across the door or windowsill.
- Trace the Caim, a protective circle, above you before sleep and say the following: "I draw the Caim around my bed. No curse shall bite, no soul be bled. From thread to flame, from root to sky, only peace and dreams shall lie."

DARK MOON PROTECTION IN THE BEDROOM

In the dark of the moon, when the sky is star cloaked and the lunar light has waned, we are most vulnerable to psychic intrusion. It is in this void, this sacred pause, that the thoughts, fears, and projections of others may creep in unbidden. To protect your bedroom sanctuary, place a piece of black tourmaline or obsidian at the bed's four corners. Anoint your temples with lavender or mugwort oil, herbs sacred to the dreaming mind and inner sight. This wards off ill will and seals the psychic field.

You can also try speaking this banishment charm aloud or whispered at the bedside: "Thoughts not mine, be gone, be still, by moon's dark grace and witch's will. Return to sender, fade from sight, I claim my peace; I seal my night. By the circle's grace and ancient decree, it is sealed."

THROUGH THE MIRROR DARKLY

Mirrors can also be helpful in protecting the bedroom during Dreamtime. Veil them with a black cloth each night. Trace a protective sigil with salt, ash, or moon water on the glass. Try placing a spirit trap—a small glass bottle with mirror shards, red thread, iron filings, and a whispered spell—near the frame. You can seal your work with these words: "No shadow pass, no watcher stay; this mirror guards, it shows my way."

Spell: Protecting the Temple

Cleansing and protecting the bedroom seals the gates. It sets the intention that only peace, healing, and truth may enter the sphere of your dreams. It is not simply about sleep but about guarding your psychic temple.

Needs

Black tourmaline, amethyst, or selenite and a small bowl of salt.

Directions

Place black tourmaline, amethyst, or selenite near your pillow or bed to protect this temple. These crystals anchor your aura, repel interference, and amplify spiritual clarity.

As you place them, say, "Stone of night, stone of day, guard my dreams, keep harm away." Place the bowl of salt beneath the bed to absorb heavy or uninvited energy. Dispose of it in the morning, offering it to the earth or washing it away so that the night's burdens do not linger.

Optional

Enhance your protection by drawing a dream sigil on parchment and placing it beneath your pillow. This sigil acts as a seal, declaring that this space is sacred and guarded to all realms.

SACRED GEOMETRY

In magickal protection, the placement of your sleeping body is never incidental. It is a geometric spell—a living compass through which your soul journeys during the liminal hours of Dreamtime. Every direction is a gate, a current, a sacred alignment. How and where you sleep becomes a map for spirit travel, ancestral communion, and psychic defence. Here are some tips:

Avoid placing your bed directly in line with the door—known in old lore as the corpse gate. This alignment draws energy out of the body, leaving you vulnerable to psychic intrusion, soul drift, and wandering spirits. Energy and spirits flow through doorways like rivers, and your bed must never lie on the path of that current.

North is the realm of the ancestors. Sleeping with your head to the north roots your soul in the earth's bones and aligns you with ancestral wisdom, grounding, and protection. Spirits who walk the ancestral roads may come to offer messages, healing, and guidance. But be mindful that this is a place of deep memory.

Cleanse and seal the space regularly with mugwort, black salt, or a sprinkling of graveyard earth to ensure clarity and peace.

East is the gate of air, of new beginnings and divine messages. Sleeping with your head to the east invites prophetic dreams, celestial guidance, and visions from the spirit. This is where the sun rises, where consciousness renews itself. Tuck a bay leaf beneath your pillow or place blue lace agate nearby to amplify clarity and higher insight.

South is the realm of fire, of vitality and transformation. Sleeping aligned to the south can stir passion, ignite courage, and protect against psychic attack, but it may also cause restlessness if not balanced. Ground the fire with a piece of garnet, or place an unlit red candle dressed with cinnamon oil at the base of your bed to seal in warmth without chaos.

West is the gate of water, the realm of emotion, intuition, and the underworld. Here, the veil is thin, and the voices of ancestors often travel through tides of dreams. Sleeping with your head to the west may awaken deep soul memories or initiate emotional healing. Guard the gateway with a bowl of moon water, sea salt, or an amethyst placed under your bed. Burn lavender or damiana (*Turnera diffusa*) as offerings to soothe the spirit realm and your soul's tides.

Above and below. Do not forget these two. What lies above your head and beneath your bed carries resonance. Clutter, mirrors, sharp objects, electronics, or disturbed currents in these planes may unravel the stability of your dream compass and leave your spirit untethered.

Cover any mirrors facing the bed, or seal them with protective sigils traced in moon water, ash, or dragon's blood oil. Mirrors are not mere glass; they are portals. Covered, they bring rest. Unsealed, they may invite the gaze of the unseen.

Suppose your home or bed rests upon land steeped in ancient memory, ley lines, forgotten burial grounds, battlefields soaked in sorrow, underground streams, or the ceaseless hum of electric pylons and Wi-Fi masts. In that case, your sanctuary may unknowingly lie atop currents of unrest. These invisible forces can stir the soul, disrupt rest, and draw forth ancestral echoes.

CRYSTALS OF THE DREAMING REALM

Crystals are the ancient keepers of earth's memory and the witch's allies in the dreamworld. For a simple protection charm and to enhance sleep, place one of the crystals from the following list under your pillow or beside your bed before you sleep at night. In the morning, cleanse the crystal with sage spray or moon water.

- *Amethyst*—Repels nightmares, enhances spiritual dreams.
- *Black Tourmaline*—Wards off psychic intrusion.
- *Hematite*—Grounds the soul and restores scattered energy.
- *Smoky Quartz*—Clears fear and helps anchor the spirit after journeying.
- *Moonstone*—Connects to lunar dreaming and psychic tides.
- *Selenite*—A soft sword of light, sweeping away residual entities.
- *Labradorite*—Conceals your energetic signature and strengthens astral clarity.

After you put them in place, breathe into them and speak: "Stone of night, stone of grace—guard my soul in Dreamtime's space."

THE DREAMTIME WARD

When the world falls silent and our bodies sleep, the spirit awakens to the vast realms of Dreamtime, where nightmares, out-of-body experiences (OBEs), and astral projection can pull us into places unknown. These realms hold immense power—but also profound peril—for within them roam spirits unbound, lingering thoughtforms, and astral parasites drawn to unguarded energy.

Without correct magickal protection, the dreamer may be vulnerable to psychic interference, energetic vampirism, spiritual attacks, or the unsettling presence of nightmare entities who feed on fear, or even servitors. Unsealed dream portals can leave the aura thin, creating cracks through which lower spirits may attach. Soul fragments may become lost in astral space, particularly after trauma or repeated night terrors. Psychic cords may be formed unconsciously through intense dream encounters—some benevolent, others binding and draining.

As witches and wise ones, we must cloak ourselves with intention and magickal protection, casting before sleep as we would before the ritual, and call upon the watchers of the threshold to guard our passage. To dream is to walk the crossroads of realms, and one must never cross unwarded.

Spell: Dreamtime Ward of the Witch

You can craft a ward to protect your dream body each night with the following spell.

Needs

Dried mugwort, a pinch of valerian root (*Valeriana officinalis*), crushed yarrow flowers, a sliver of black tourmaline or obsidian, a drop of lavender oil on a cloth, a small black or deep blue pouch, and red or black thread.

Directions

Place the ingredients in a small black or deep blue pouch. Tie the pouch closed with red or black thread, sealing it with a whispered incantation: "By thread and thorn, by moon and mist, no shadow may enter, no serpent twist. My dream is mine, my will is clear. Guardians of night, draw ever near."

This Dreamtime ward may also be hung above the bed, laid at the threshold of the sleeping space, or recharged under the full moon. Replace the herbs at each Sabbat or when dreams become clouded.

THE WITCH'S DREAMTIME SHIELD

To the awakened witch, dreams are not passive—they are portals, scrolls of prophecy, and battlegrounds alike. Just as we cast circles in the waking world, so must we shield the spirit before slumber, cloaking ourselves in sigils, stones, and lunar intention.

Magickal practitioners should generally weave a dream shield—a psychic ward created before sleep using enchanted tools such as crystals, sacred symbols, planetary timing, and spirit allies.

In some occult traditions, the triangle of manifestation—commonly used to summon—is reversed to form a triangle of banishment; marked in chalk, ash (*Fraxinus excelsior*), or bloodroot powder (*Sanguinaria canadensis*); and hidden beneath the bed. You can strengthen its power further by anointing the triangle with Saturn oil or placing a shard of lead at its centre. Doing so will make it a ward of capture, anchoring the space and keeping dream interlopers at bay.

When you do dream shielding spells, work on Saturn's day (Saturday) to align with boundary magick and use the moon as a guide, depending on why you are creating the shield. Work on a waxing moon for deep sight, ancestral wisdom, and dream retrieval and on a waning moon for banishing nightmares, energetic closure, and severing astral cords.

You can also create a protective talisman of onyx or hematite and invoke Archangel Cassiel, the watcher of Saturn's gate, to enhance the power of your shield.

The shield itself might be visualised as a silver sphere, a serpent of light, or a veil of obsidian mist drawn around the body, invoked with whispered enchantments known only to the witch.

Ritual: Your Dream Shield

Following is a ritual to help you create your Dreamtime shield. Before starting, make sure you've chosen a sigil or rune to use for protection and have a protective dream talisman, if desired.

Needs

Dried angelica, hyssop, or damiana and protection oil.

Directions

First set the space. Burn the herbs to thin the veil and call in guardianship. Anoint your third eye or heart centre with the protective oil and trace a personal sigil or rune of sealing to align with your inner gate.

Perform one of the suggested shielding workings listed earlier. Visualise your shield as you lie in bed. Then seal your rite with this: "With shadow sealed and circle cast, no force shall enter, and none shall pass. Through ancient rites and sacred fire, only truth may cross this wire."

Never forget the power of your name. Speak your full magickal name before you sleep—declaring your sovereignty in the realms beyond.

NIGHTMARES, OBES, AND ASTRAL PROJECTION

Within the Dreamtime, the soul does not merely rest—it travels. For witches and sensitives, the dream state becomes a gateway to the astral planes, where the spirit may unhook from the body and explore other realms of consciousness. These experiences are known as OBEs (out-of-body experiences) or astral projection, and while they can be profound initiations, they are not without risk.

In an OBE or astral journey, your spirit body—also called the eidolon, dream double, or astral twin—leaves the physical vessel and moves freely in non-ordinary dimensions. These may include the lower astral, where unanchored energies, confused spirits, and shadow entities reside, or the higher astral, where soul wisdom, spirit allies, and celestial temples of light may be accessed.

Nightmares, in this context, are not always random. They may be:

- Psychic attacks from unseen forces or people.
- Echoes of unresolved emotional trauma.
- Shadow trials initiated by your unconscious.
- Encounters with astral parasites or spirits that feed on fear.

For the unwarded dreamer, these can manifest as terror, paralysis, or exhaustion upon waking. What appears as a bad dream may, in truth, be a visitation, a lesson, or a challenge. And like all liminal gateways, the astral realm must be entered with reverence, ritual, and protection.

For deeper protection against these forces, incorporating ritual baths with purifying herbs like mugwort or rosemary before bed can cleanse your aura and prepare you for restful sleep. Additionally, performing a cleansing ritual in your bedroom, such as burning sage or frankincense, ensures your sleeping space remains a sanctuary of protection.

EMERGENCY BANISHING RITE

If you awaken from a nightmare or spiritual disturbance at night in the Dreamtime, immediately name the dream aloud and state it has no claim on your energy. Then clap your hands three times or ring a spirit bell to break the connection and thread. Mist your space with moon water, witch hazel, and rosemary. Seal the rite, saying, "No claim shall linger, no bond shall hold."

Spell: Dream Satchel for Nightmares and Other Disruptions

If nightmares or spiritual unrest is present, craft a dream satchel to help.

Needs

Dried lavender, chamomile, mugwort, and rose petals in equal quantities; a small satchel.

Directions

Place the dried herbs in your satchel and tie it shut. These plants form a hedge of light and scent around your soul, guiding you into peaceful, protected dreaming. Hang the satchel near your bed or place it under your pillow. Then whisper, "Herbs of peace and light, protect my sleep throughout the night."

ALLIES AND GUARDIANS OF SLEEP

Just as we would never open a circle without casting sacred space, so must we never enter the Dreamtime unguarded. Allies and guardians are essential to navigate the veils safely and return with our power intact.

Before sleep, you can invoke your night guardians, spirits, deities, or ancestors who will watch over you as you dream. Doing so is simple. Light a candle and call to your guardian to ask for their protection. If you don't have a particular guardian to call, you can say, "Guardians of the darkened skies, I call to thee with sacred cries. Protect my soul through night's deep veil and guard my spirit should I sail. No harm shall come, no fear shall rise, shield me from all unseen eyes. My dreams are guarded and sealed by the circle's power and ancient decree."

Dreamtime Protection Rite

Within the folds of night, when spirit unlaces from flesh and drifts into the veiled realms, this rite shall cloak you in magickal protection. It is a spell to shield against nightmares, banish all meddling spirits, and ensure only those of light may walk with you through the gates of Dreamtime and beyond.

Needs

One black candle (to invoke the protective flame), a shard of hematite or a piece of obsidian (to anchor and absorb interference), a pinch of dried mugwort or lavender (to soften the veil and call dream wisdom), and a length of silver ribbon or thread (to tether the spell to lunar guardianship).

Directions

As twilight deepens, cleanse the space around your bed with breath, sound, or sacred smoke. Lay your tools before you like offerings on an altar.

Place the black candle at the edge of your dream threshold—your bedside or beneath the window where moonlight pours. Encircle its base with the chosen herb, letting the scent awaken your soul's remembering.

Take the hematite or obsidian in both hands. Close your eyes. Breathe into it. Feel it pulse with silent strength. Speak to it in the old tongue of thought: "Guard me from those who travel with shadowed intent. Let no echo of malice find me in sleep."

Now, light the candle and say aloud, "By shadowed stone and sacred flame, I seal my soul in the Dreamtime's name. No darkness may cross, no whisper may bind; only truth and light in dreams I find. By lunar thread and witch's will, let the veil be strong, and the night is still."

Wind the silver thread slowly around the stone as if winding the moon's light into its core. This binds the spell to the ancient tides and guardians of night.

Place the stone beneath your pillow or beside your dreaming brow. Let the candle burn in silence—or snuff it gently, whispering, "It is done."

Sleep now, witch of the veil. The gates are now guarded.

PROTECTORS IN THE HIDDEN REALMS

As we drift beyond the body, we become accessible to energies that do not belong to us—some ancestral, others parasitic, and some simply curious. To navigate these realms with safety and sovereignty, we do not go alone, for two great protectors of the Dreamtime walk with us: the shadow guardian and the shadow familiar.

THE DREAM GUARDIAN

A dream guardian is an external protector—a being of spirit, deity, ancestor, or ancient intelligence assigned to you across life times. This guardian walks at the edge of your dream temple, shielding your soul during OBEs, astral travel, or deep dreaming. They are invoked to hold space, stand watch, and deflect spiritual interference. Often appearing as cloaked guides, light beings, or animal spirits, they are called with sacred intention and loyalty to your soul's path.

CALLING THE DREAM GUARDIAN

Before sleep, invoke your night guardians—spirits, deities, ancestors, or your dream guardian, a protective being who walks beside your soul across lifetimes. They may appear as shadow animals, ancestral spirits, or ancient guides cloaked in silence and starlight.

Some will appear as wolves, owls, serpents, or other familiars of the night. Others may be formless yet deeply known to your soul, appearing only in dreams and visions when called. These guardians walk the liminal roads, deflecting harm and guiding your spirit along its rightful path.

To summon them before sleep, light a candle—black, silver, or indigo—and speak this incantation as a sacred key to the dream gates: "Guardians of the darkened skies, I call to thee with sacred cries. Protect my soul through night's deep veil, and guard my spirit should I sail. No harm shall come, no fear shall rise; shield me from all unseen eyes. Dream Guardian, walk close by me—through shadowed paths and mystery. My dreams are guarded and sealed, by the circle's power and ancient decree."

THE SHADOW FAMILIAR

By contrast, a shadow familiar arises from within. It is born not of calling but of remembering, emerging from the hidden parts of your soul reclaimed through shadow work, ancestral healing, and profound transformation. This being carries your buried instincts, primal gifts, and fierce wisdom. It does not stand at the edge of your circle—it walks beside you in the dark, silent and watchful, ready to strike when something dares cross your path uninvited.

While a dream guardian shields from without, the shadow familiar protects from within. Together, they offer the witch unmatched power in navigating the unseen.

If you walk with a shadow familiar, invite it into your dreams. These spirits arise from the deep self, forged through shadow work, trauma healing, and soul retrieval. They are primal, protective, and wise beyond words. They silence what lurks in the dark and walk beside the witch as watchers in the void.

GUARDIAN OF THE HIDDEN SELF

A shadow familiar is not merely a companion spirit—it is an extension of your deeper self, born from the spaces where your wounds, power, and wisdom intertwine. Unlike traditional familiars who often appear in physical or etheric animal forms for aid and guidance, the shadow familiar arises through deep inner work—particularly shadow work, soul retrieval, and ancestral reclamation.

It is a being forged in the crucible of your unconscious, carrying the instincts, protection, and primal energy that the conscious mind often fears or suppresses. These familiars are fierce, loyal, and wise. They walk silently through realms others dare not enter, protecting the witch from spiritual predators, energetic parasites, and interference in the unseen.

They may appear in dreams as black animals—wolves, owls, serpents, panthers—or shape-shift between forms. Some come cloaked in shadow, faceless yet deeply known. Others bear markings of your past lives or soul lineage.

To meet your shadow familiar, you must be willing to face yourself—your rage, your sorrow, your lost power—and embrace it, for they are not summoned like servants. They remember you before you remember yourself.

In the Dreamtime, your shadow familiar becomes your most potent guardian. While spirit guides may offer light and ancestors may offer wisdom, the shadow familiar stands at the gate, silent and alert, ensuring that nothing crosses your dream temple without your will.

You do not command them. You walk with them. And in walking together, your soul becomes whole.

Elemental Guardian Protection Rite

To restore harmony and protection, anchor the space with elemental guardians.

Needs

Four iron nails, four copper coils, and four shungite stones.

Directions

Place the iron nails in each corner of the room or beneath the bed's four corners to ward off restless spirits and ground the spirit's body. Next, place the copper coils in the same place. They conduct and redirect chaotic energy, harmonising the flow between earth and sky.

Finally, place the shungite stones, forged of ancient carbon, in each corner to absorb electromagnetic frequencies, purify shadow energy, and shield the dream body from geopathic stress.

Whisper this incantation as you place each object: "By earth's strong bones and time's deep tide, let all unrest now step aside. With iron, copper, shungite stone, I claim this space; I make it home."

Finish by visualising a shimmering sphere of golden or silvery light settling over your room—calm, clear, and sealed.

Complete the compass by calling your dream guardian or shadow familiar to walk you beyond the veil.

These guides hold the map of your soul's terrain and will walk beside you if called with reverence.

When you go to sleep, speak this whisper before sleep: "Compass turn and spirit see, stars and roots align with me. From north to west and south to east, let my soul in peace be released."

Now sleep not as a wanderer but as a wise one who knows the unseen and how to ward against unwanted intruders.

MORNING'S LIGHT

As the light of morning returns and the soul is gathered back from its nocturnal path, the work of the magickal practitioner is not yet done. While the journey may close, the chamber in which it began must now be sealed, tended, and warded for the following passage. Just as we return our spirit to the body, so must we cloak the space from which we departed, fortifying it with stones, symbols, and ancestral safeguards. This is not only the art of dreaming but the craft of magickal protection, of weaving spells into thread, placement, and purpose. What follows are the sacred tools and final rites that anchor your dreamwork in power and ensure the veil remains guarded until your will next opens it.

Morning Rite: Calling the Spirit Home

When we journey beyond the veil at night—whether through OBEs, astral travel, or deep dream magick—part of our energy may remain extended. Without conscious return, we may wake feeling disoriented, fragmented, or energetically drained. This morning rite ensures your soul is recalled, sealed, and restored.

Needs

A piece of hematite, smoky quartz, or black tourmaline; a shallow bowl of warm water or moon water; and a pinch of salt or a drop of rosemary oil.

Directions

Upon waking, sit upright or stand at the edge of your bed. Hold the crystal in your dominant hand and place the bowl before you. Add the salt or oil to the water, stirring clockwise. As you stir, say, "Waters of waking, cleanse and restore; call me home from every shore."

Take three deep breaths. On each exhale, visualise silver threads returning from the dream realm, drawing back into your heart, crown, and root. Dip your fingers into the water and touch it to your third eye, heart, and feet, saying, "By water's kiss and crystal's weight, I close the gate. I seal my fate. Returned, restored, my spirit whole, I walk awake in power and soul."

Place the crystal on your altar or the earth for grounding. Respectfully dispose of the water outdoors or down the drain. Repeat this final affirmation: "Upon waking, I call all parts of my spirit home, sealed and whole beneath the sun once more."

17
BANEFUL MAGICK: ADDRESSING CURSES, HEXES, AND PSYCHIC ATTACKS

I have spent over thirty-five years working in the art of magickal protection and have faced countless instances of ill will. These are not relics of ancient history nor folklore. They happen far more often than people realise. Until now, I have shared a winding path of protection magick woven with empowerment and heightened self-awareness. I have shown you how to call upon unseen allies, harness the power of intention, and weave protection into the very fabric of our magickal lives.

But now, the path darkens. I will discuss how to counter the forces that harm, disrupt, and drain. Baneful magick, in the form of curses, hexes, jinxes, and ill will, possesses immense power in the hands of those who wield it, whether intentionally or through emotional unrest. Yet you should not enter these shadows unprepared. To face this shadow, you must first acknowledge it. You enter a realm where fear, anger, envy, and unseen forces attempt to manipulate or weaken you. But with knowledge comes power, and with awareness, you can rise above. It is time to shine light into these hidden places and claim your strength.

Remember, the hidden darkness comes in many forms, from thoughtforms that feed off anxiety to shadow entities lurking at the edge of our perception. Protecting yourself requires constant awareness, regular cleansing, and a profound understanding of your energy and the forces that surround you. The unseen forces are subtle, but they are not invincible. With the proper knowledge, vigilance, and magickal practice, you can fortify your life against these entities and stay empowered in your craft.

BANEFUL MAGICK AND PROTECTION

Baneful magick is sometimes necessary, or using magick to defend against evil forces or individuals with harmful intent. In the face of injustice, oppression, or psychic attacks, baneful magick can be a vital tool for ensuring your safety.

While it is crucial to approach such workings cautiously, the art of baneful magick can offer significant protection when used ethically and responsibly. This includes binding harmful people or energies, reversing hostile intentions, or sending destructive energies back to their source. Here is a simple binding spell to prevent a harmful person from causing further damage.

Spell: Halting Harm

This binding spell is a powerful way to neutralise harmful energies while maintaining your ethical responsibility to avoid harm.

Needs

A black ribbon or string, a piece of parchment with the person's name written on it, and a black candle.

Directions

Light the black candle, focusing on the person or force you wish to bind. Take the parchment and begin wrapping the black ribbon around it, saying, "By this ribbon, I bind your power; you shall not harm from this hour. No ill intent, no dark desire, shall you cross my path or rise any higher." Now visualise their harmful energy being tied and bound, unable to affect you or anyone else. When you've finished wrapping the ribbon, either bury it in the earth or store it in a safe place where it will remain undisturbed.

CURSES, HEXES, JINXES

Curses, hexes, and jinxes, as well as the evil force of ill will, exist within the fabric of human nature. Jealousy, anger, and fear are the driving emotions behind these acts. These forces, whether consciously or unconsciously wielded, can create ripples of harm in a person's life, affecting their mental, emotional, and physical well-being. In my line of work, I have seen this time and again. It's incredible how people do not realise how powerful and affected they can be and how it can affect those targeted!

If you understand the implements of defensive magick, build your wards, cast your protective spells, and maintain your shields, you can safeguard yourself. Protection magick is not about avoiding the world's dark forces but about meeting them with power and resilience.

IDENTIFYING A CURSE, HEX, OR JINX

Over the years, countless people have shared a familiar story with me: "I've been cursed!" they tell me, convinced that their string of bad luck or personal misfortune is the result of someone else's malicious intent. But when I've looked deeper into the situation, more often than not, they haven't been cursed at all. Instead, they're experiencing the effects of a jinx, ill will, or even a run of unfortunate events.

If you're dealing with a curse, the symptoms are persistent and unyielding, affecting not just one area of your life but multiple. Bad luck, health issues, relationship breakdowns, and financial loss all occur simultaneously or in rapid succession. A cursed person often feels as though they are being systematically worn down, as if an invisible weight is pressing on their life, making everything more complicated than it should be. Curses can last for years or even generations until the curse is broken. If your misfortunes seem deeply embedded and ongoing despite your efforts to turn things around, you may be dealing with a curse. Look for patterns that are unexplainable for mundane reasons.

A hex targets specific aspects of your career, love life, or health and are typically designed to create chaos or discomfort in a particular area rather than affecting your entire life. Do you have sudden disruptions in one part of your life, such as a job loss, relationship arguments, or a streak of bad luck in a specific situation? The effects of a hex are sharp and noticeable and localised. Hexes can last for days, weeks, or months but are not designed to linger indefinitely. If the adverse effects seem focused on one area of your life and appear suddenly, you might be dealing with a hex.

Jinxes bring a series of small, irritating misfortunes rather than life-altering problems. Have you had any annoying but relatively minor setbacks, such as losing your keys, missing appointments, or minor financial inconveniences? Have you had frustrating problems that may come in waves, but aren't catastrophic? Jinxes typically fade away on their own after a short period, lasting days or weeks. If you're experiencing a string of bad luck that feels more like a temporary irritation than something serious, it's likely a jinx.

ILL WILL AND THE EVIL EYE

When people come to me convinced that they've been cursed, I always start by asking about the symptoms. Most of the time, what they are experiencing is the result of negative thoughts or minor ill will rather than a full-blown curse. Knowing the difference is essential, as the solutions for each situation vary greatly. A simple energy cleansing might be enough to dispel a jinx or ill will, while breaking a curse requires far more powerful and targeted magick.

Ill will and the evil eye are often rooted in jealousy, envy, or anger. These energies are typically not cast through formal magickal rituals, but they can still have an effect. Ill will is the negative energy someone directs toward you, often unconsciously, through thoughts of negativity, jealousy, or resentment. Symptoms include feeling drained, low energy, or experiencing random bad luck after interacting with someone with ill feelings toward you. The evil eye, in particular, is said to bring about bad luck, fatigue, or even illness. Ill will, or the evil eye, can affect you as long as the person holds negative feelings toward you. It can be fleeting or persistent, depending on the situation.

ANCESTRAL CURSES

Ancestral curses are among the most powerful and enduring forms of malevolent magick, often passed down through generations within a family line. These curses can arise from deeply traumatic events, such as a witch or practitioner of the craft who, upon facing execution or persecution, curses those responsible, vowing that their descendants will suffer for their actions. Such curses can also result from broken oaths, familial betrayals, or acts of great malice that bind future generations to the curse.

Ancestral curses are not always easy to detect, but they tend to manifest as recurring patterns within a family. Misfortune, illness, or relationship breakdowns that persist across generations can be a crucial indicator of an ancestral curse. Often, these curses affect multiple members of a family line, with each generation experiencing similar hardships or failures despite their efforts to break free.

HOW TO DETECT AN ANCESTRAL CURSE

One of the most evident signs of an ancestral curse is a repeating cycle of misfortune that affects multiple generations. These can include consistent financial struggles, untimely deaths, infertility, or broken relationships that seem to mirror the experiences of parents, grandparents, and even great-grandparents. Ancestral curses are often tied to the family's energetic field. If you feel an unexplainable heaviness or sense of doom that seems to have no personal cause but is linked to your family, this could be a sign of an ancestral curse.

Sometimes, a family will have a known history of trauma or betrayal that has resulted in a curse. If your ancestors were involved in witch trials, brutal acts of war, or other violent, traumatic events, there may be a curse tied to those actions. Breaking an ancestral curse requires more than individual cleansing or protection. It often involves working with ancestors, healing past trauma, and performing rituals designed to cut ties to the negative energies carried forward through the family line.

SACRED TOOLS FOR BINDING AND BANISHMENT

In magickal work, particular objects from the natural world carry immense power when used in binding and banishment spells. These items are not only protective, but they also help contain or repel negative energy and harmful forces. Incorporating these sacred objects into your spells and rituals allows you to create powerful boundaries, lock away unwanted influences, and defend your personal space. Drawing from the earth's natural gifts, these items strengthen protection, ensuring your magickal defences are firm and lasting. Below is a list of the most common tools for banishment:

- Animal symbols represent the protective qualities of specific animals, such as ravens, wolves, or owls. They are used in charms or as physical representations to guard the home or sacred spaces and are invoked for guidance, spiritual defence, and protection.
- Blackthorn or hawthorn thorns are used in banishing or binding spells to pierce and drive away negative energy. Strong for protective charms to guard against psychic attacks. It can be carried for personal protection against curses.
- Bones and skulls are symbols of ancestral protection and wisdom. Used in rituals to connect with spirits

or ancestors for protection. Placed on altars or in homes to guard against hostile forces.

- Bramble vines are associated with protection and binding. Used in spells to entangle and trap harmful energies. It is vital for creating boundaries and guarding against unwanted influences.
- Horseshoes are hung above doorways to guard against bad luck and negative energy. Used as a protective charm to ensure safety and harmony in the home.
- Iron nails are used in binding spells to nail down or contain hostile forces. Often buried in doorsteps or placed around homes for protection. Strong for sealing away harmful energies.
- Keys are symbols of protection and access to hidden knowledge. Used in charms and spells to lock away negative energy or open paths to safety. Often placed near doors or windows for protection of the home.
- Knotted red thread is tied into knots for binding and banishment spells. Often carried or placed in spaces for long-lasting protection. Used to trap negative energy or spirits and prevent them from returning. Vital for deflecting harmful intentions.
- Witch's balls are hung on doors or windows to ward off negative energy. Used to break up stagnant energy and clear spaces. Strong for protection against unwanted spirits and harmful influences.

WHAT TO DO WHEN YOU'VE BEEN CURSED OR HEXED

Discovering that you've been cursed or hexed can feel overwhelming, but it's important to remember that curses and hexes are not invincible, no matter how powerful. You can break the curse and fortify yourself against future attacks with the right knowledge and magickal protection. Here's what to do if you believe you've been cursed or hexed.

The first step is to remove any lingering negative energy. Cleansing your aura and living space helps eliminate the residual effects of dark magick. Use smoke cleansing with black smoke, cedar, or rue (*Ruta graveolens*). Take a ritual bath infused with salt, protective herbs, or oils like rosemary or hyssop. You can also use sounds such as bells or clapping to clear stagnant energy. Once cleaned, it's time to break the curse or hex. This is an active process and may require several steps depending on the severity.

MIRROR SPELL

One effective way to break a curse is to reflect the harmful energy back to its source using a mirror spell. Place a small mirror facing outward in your home, ensuring that any negative energy directed at you is reflected away.

REVERSAL SPELL

Reversal spells are another powerful method. These rituals work by turning the curse back on the caster. A simple reversal involves carving your name and intention into a black candle, anointing it with protective oils like black pepper or dragon's blood and burning it while focusing on reversing the curse.

BINDING RITUAL

In some cases, it may be necessary to perform a binding ritual to prevent the person who cursed or hexed you from doing further harm. A binding spell can stop the individual from sending additional negative energy your way. A straightforward method involves writing their name on a piece of paper, wrapping it in black thread, placing it in a jar of salt, and sealing it to prevent further harm.

REGULAR PROTECTION PRACTICES

Cleansing and breaking a curse is not the end of the journey. Maintaining regular protection rituals is crucial for protecting yourself from future magickal attacks. Incorporate protective crystals, herbs, and talismans into your daily routine. Wear amulets charged with protection spells and renew your wards and sigils regularly to keep your defences strong.

PSYCHIC ATTACKS

Psychic attacks are another form of harm that don't always involve ritual or spellwork like curses or hexes. Instead, these attacks come from intense negative thoughts, emotions, or intentions directed at you by someone else. The energy behind a psychic attack can come from anger, jealousy, or resentment, even if the person sending it is unaware of the damage they are causing.

While a curse or hex is typically an intentional act, a psychic attack can be unintentional and often happens when someone harbours intense negative emotions toward you. These attacks can manifest as feelings of being drained, sudden mood swings, anxiety, or even physical symptoms such as headaches or fatigue. The effects of a psychic attack may be just as debilitating as a curse, especially if the person directing the attack holds significant emotional power over you.

EXPLORING PSYCHIC ATTACKS

Psychic attacks are far more subtle than the physical ones we experience, yet they can leave just as much of a mark, often without us even realising where the damage is coming from. A psychic attack happens when negative energy is directed toward you, consciously or unconsciously. This energy can come from harmful thoughts, curses, jealousy, or ill wishes. While we may not see this energy with our eyes, we can feel its effects deeply as it seeps into our energy field, draining our life force, clouding our minds, and stirring chaos in our emotional and spiritual centres.

Recognising a psychic attack can be tricky because the symptoms are often subtle, but here are some common signs: feeling inexplicably drained, tired, or anxious after being around a particular person; sudden mood swings, irritability, or depression that seem to come from nowhere; a sense of heaviness, as if you are carrying someone else's emotional burden; and unexplained physical symptoms such as headaches, nausea, or a feeling of pressure.

DEFENDING AGAINST PSYCHIC ATTACKS

The good news is that psychic attacks can be deflected with regular cleansing and protection practices. Keeping your energy field strong and setting physical and energetic boundaries can prevent these attacks from affecting you. Here's a powerful, all-encompassing spell designed to reverse, banish, and neutralise curses, hexes, ill will, and psychic attacks. It uses blackthorn salt for maximum potency.

Spell: Blackthorn Banishing

This spell is for when you must rid yourself of curses, hexes, ill will, or psychic attacks. It calls upon the power of blackthorn, a potent protector and wielder of dark magick, to strike down any harmful energy sent your way and banish it back to its source. As a purifier, blackthorn salt ensures that what is removed is cleansed thoroughly, leaving no trace behind.

Needs

A blackthorn wand or a blackthorn branch (if unavailable, use a strong piece of wood), blackthorn thorns (if unavailable, use needles), salt (coarse sea salt or blackthorn salt), a black bang bang candle (for reversal), dragon's blood oil or a protective oil of choice, and a mirror (optional, for added reflection of energy).

Directions

Begin by cleansing the area with smoke from sage, rosemary, or your preferred cleansing herb. Visualise any negative energy lifting and dissipating as the smoke fills the space. Create a circle of salt on the floor or altar. Place the black candle at the centre of the circle and anoint it with the dragon's blood oil, charging it with your intent to reverse and banish any harmful energy sent your way. Hold your blackthorn wand or branch firmly in your power hand. As you do, imagine it charging with ancient power, ready to strike down any ill intent or energy clinging to you.

Repeat the following incantation as you focus on the candle and hold your blackthorn wand: "By thorn and salt, by fire and stone, all that was sent shall be undone. Reverse the curse, hex, or attack; with blackthorn's power, send it back. No ill shall harm, no spell shall stay, by this circle's power, I clear the way. Gone are the shadows, banished the ill, by my will alone, peace shall stand still."

Using the blackthorn thorn (or needle), prick the black candle near its base. As the wax melts, visualise the curse or ill will being pierced and drained of its power, dissolving into nothingness. Allow the candle to burn completely. When it's finished, take the remaining salt and any leftover wax and dispose of it outside your home, far from your space. If you've used a mirror, cover it with a cloth to deactivate its energy.

THE POWER BEHIND THE ATTACK

From my experience, it takes an exceptional wizard, magickian, high priestess, or witch of the highest calibre to cast a curse and sustain its energy. Cursing or hexing someone is not lightly undertaken; it requires immense focus, power, and often deep reservoirs of anger or hatred. This kind of magick drains not only the person it's directed at but also the practitioner themself.

For a curse to persist, it draws energy from the one who cast it, which means that the longer it lingers, the more it weakens the sender. This is why, as soon as you become aware of the negative energy surrounding you—whether it's a curse, hex, or psychic attack—you can use defensive magick to deflect and reverse it. Knowing the source of the energy can be empowering, and as

I've learned, nine times out of ten, it comes from someone we already know.

However, it's not always the seen or the obvious that we must guard against. More often, the unseen forces, the subtle energies lurking just beyond our conscious awareness, require the greatest vigilance. This is where our intuition, inner knowing, and magickal abilities come into play. When we remain grounded in our magickal protection, we can shield ourselves from the known and the unknown, ensuring that no harm touches us.

THOUGHTFORMS AND ENERGETIC PARASITES

Thoughtforms, sometimes called tulpas or egregores, are entities created through focused thoughts or emotions. They can be intentional or accidental, arising from repeated negative thinking patterns, fear, or collective societal energies. These thoughtforms can latch onto individuals, feeding off their energy and amplifying negative emotions like anxiety, anger, or sadness. Regular cleansing of your aura, strong mental boundaries, and focused intent on dispelling negative energies can help dissolve these entities.

ASTRAL PARASITES

Astral parasites exist in the unseen realms and often attach themselves to individuals who frequently engage in spiritual work, such as astral projection, journeying, or mediumship. These entities feed on energy and can drain life force, leaving one feeling fatigued, unfocused, or emotionally overwhelmed. Astral protection rituals are crucial, such as creating energetic shields before journeying or calling on astral guardians. Daily grounding and cleansing after spiritual work are equally important.

WALK-INS

Walk-ins are entities that enter the body of a person during moments of trauma, vulnerability, or extreme emotional distress. These entities can subtly influence the person's thoughts, actions, and emotions, often leading to personality changes or self-destructive behaviour. Shadow work, regular aura cleansing, and soul retrieval rituals can help restore personal sovereignty. Psychic shielding and warding against spiritual intrusions are also vital.

SPIRIT ATTACHMENTS

Spirits, whether earthbound or malevolent, can attach themselves to people, especially those in states of grief, addiction, or emotional vulnerability. These attachments often drain energy and subtly manipulate thoughts or emotions, causing a person to feel out of control. Symptoms include unexplained negative emotions, sudden cravings or addictions, and an ongoing sense of unease or not being alone. Spirit banishment rituals, protective sigils, and working with a trusted spiritual guide to remove attachments can also help keep malevolent spirits at bay. Regular offerings to ancestral spirits and protection deities can also help.

DREAM INVADERS

Dark entities that invade our dream space—often referred to as dream demons, nightmares, or incubi—can manipulate or torment us during sleep, leading to restless nights, emotional instability, or a general feeling of unease upon waking. These entities thrive in the liminal spaces of the subconscious mind. Dream wards—such as protective herbs under the pillow, enchanted dream catchers, and invoking astral guardians before sleep—can block these entities from entering the dream realm.

PSYCHIC VAMPIRES

Psychic vampires feed on the energy of others, often without their knowledge. These can be people in your life or unseen entities that latch onto your aura, draining your life force to fuel themselves. Psychic vampires often leave their victims feeling drained, irritable, or unable to function after encounters. Psychic shields, cutting energetic cords, and fortifying your aura through visualisation and intent effectively block these entities. Amulets of protection, such as black tourmaline or obsidian, are also helpful.

ENTITY-INDUCED ADDICTIONS

Certain dark entities are known to attach themselves to individuals struggling with addictions, whether they be substances, unhealthy behaviours, or toxic relationships. These entities thrive on the repeated emotional and physical drain caused by addiction, making it harder for the person to break free. If affected, you might feel intensified cravings, hopelessness, and like you're trapped in destructive patterns. Spiritual detoxification rituals, healing spells for emotional wounds, and calling on spirit guides or deities assist in breaking free from these entities.

THE EVIL EYE

Although the evil eye is often thought of as intentional, there are times when it's cast unconsciously through jealousy or envy. Its energy can cause misfortune, ill health, or emotional turmoil, subtly working its way into your life without you realising the source. Wearing protective charms or amulets—such as the Eye of Horus, the hamsa, or even a reflective mirror talisman—can deflect the harmful energies of the evil eye. Regular protection spells are also essential to keep jealousy and envy at bay.

SHADOW ENTITIES

Shadow entities are dark beings often appearing at the edge of perception—in doorways, corners, or during sleep paralysis. These beings feed on fear and anxiety and often leave a lingering sense of unease or dread. Creating protective wards around your home, invoking guardian spirits, and using protective incantations before bed can help prevent shadow entities from gaining a foothold.

BASIC WAYS TO GUARD YOUR LIFE FORCE

While psychic defence targets the harmful energy being sent your way, energetic defence focuses on fortifying your spirit, life force, and connection to the divine. Just as a house must have strong walls to keep intruders out, your spirit must have solid boundaries and shields to ensure that nothing can penetrate your energy.

BASIC PRACTICES OF DEFENCE

Energetic defence starts with awareness. Like in karate, the more attuned you are to the energies around you, the quicker you can respond to an attack. Pay attention to how you feel in different environments, around certain people, and during certain times. If you notice your energy shifting, take action to cleanse and protect yourself.

Here are the essential practices for building strong defences and guarding your life force against psychic attacks.

SHIELDING WITH VISUALISATION

Begin with your shield. Visualise a protective barrier of light around you, whether shimmering gold, bright white, or obsidian's deep, impenetrable black. This shield should be flexible but strong, moving with you throughout your day and sealing any vulnerabilities.

INVOCATION FOR PSYCHIC AND SPIRITUAL SHIELDING

Use this invocation to help shield and protect: "By my will and the power within, I call forth this shield, solid and unbroken. No harm shall pass, and no ill shall enter. I am protected, sealed, and whole by the light that surrounds and guards my soul."

CLEANSING RITUALS

Monthly cleansing of your aura and space is vital to keep harmful energy at bay. Use smoke from sage, rosemary, or mugwort to clear your aura. Bathe with blackthorn salt and protective herbs to purify your energy centres, ensuring your spirit remains clean and resilient. And either when cleansing your aura or bathing, say, "By smoke and salt, I cleanse this space; no shadow may linger, and no ill has a place. My aura is bright, my spirit clear. All harm is gone, and no fear draws near."

RETURN-TO-SENDER SPELLS

When you feel a direct psychic attack, a return-to-sender spell can effectively send that harmful energy back to its source. This type of spell doesn't harm the sender but redirects the energy to its origin, ensuring it does not linger with you. Say, "The energy you send, I send back thrice. No harm shall touch, and no ill shall suffice. By mirror and light, I shield and reflect; your intent is returned, no cause to affect."

HOW THOUGHTS SHAPE ENERGETIC SHIELDS

The power of the spoken word is undeniable in magick, but even unspoken thoughts hold immense potential. Thoughts are the seeds of reality, and when left unchecked, they can weaken our defences, much like an ill-spoken word. On the contrary, intentional words and thoughts are the bricks that build the fortress around our energy. Imagine every word and thought you speak and feel as part of the woven threads of your magickal protection. Your energetic shield grows more vital when you focus on strength, resilience, and empowerment. But if your thoughts slip into fear, anger, or self-doubt, those threads become frayed, leaving gaps in your protection.

To reinforce your energetic shields, you can use daily affirmations and spoken words of power that serve as a protective mantra. Just say, "My words are woven, strong and clear, building a shield that draws me near. I am safe, I am whole, protected by my sacred soul. No harm shall pass, no ill shall stay, my shield is sealed throughout the day." Speak this affirmation every morning, weaving it into your routine. As you do so, envision a radiant bubble of protective energy surrounding you. Visualise it is growing stronger with every word you speak, solidifying your defences against harmful energies or psychic attacks.

BEING PRAYED AGAINST

One of the lesser-discussed forms of psychic attack is the experience of being prayed against. This form of spiritual interference is especially harmful when it comes from those who consciously or unconsciously wish to use their spiritual practice to manipulate your path or weaken your defences. These prayers aim to control or limit your power and are often motivated by fear, jealousy, or an opposing belief system. While prayer is typically seen as a positive force, praying against someone is a violation of spiritual boundaries, and as witches, we must reclaim our power from such interference.

The impact of being prayed against can manifest as a slow drain on your energy, an unshakable feeling of unease, or sudden obstacles in your path that seem to come out of nowhere. You may feel blocked in your magickal practice or disconnected from your intuition as the prayer's energy pulls at your essence like invisible chains.

Ritual: Breaking Free from Spiritual Interference

This ritual severs the ties of unwanted spiritual interference, ensuring you regain control over your path and power.

Needs

A white candle for purity and cleansing, a black tourmaline crystal for protection, and sea salt for cleansing.

Directions

Light the white candle, hold the black tourmaline in your hand, and say, "No prayer, no spell shall bind my will; my spirit is free; my soul stands still. I break the chains, I sever the ties; I am my own under moonlit skies. No force shall sway my magick's course, by my will and sacred source." Sprinkle the salt around you in a circle, symbolising the purification of your energy. Allow the candle to burn down completely.

18
ADVANCED PROTECTION WORK

This chapter crosses a threshold. It leads the practitioner beyond foundational spellcraft and into the arcane sanctum of advanced magickal protection—a realm where your soul becomes both sentinel and sigil. Here, the magick is not just protective but strategic, sovereign, and deeply spiritual. These workings are not for the newly awakened or the lightly curious. They are for the seasoned witch whose light has grown so steady and strong that it casts a shadow across planes, drawing the gaze of spirits, energies, and forces not of this world. In this space, the witch's compass is a directional tool and a sacred geometry that aligns your spirit across worlds. Every rite in this chapter was forged in the crucible of experience, tested under pressure, and shaped by the silence of the unseen. This magick fortifies your dreamscape, wards your bloodline, and binds the breach between worlds.

My journey into this hidden realm began when I was just thirteen years old, taken under the wing of Swein Macdonald—the Original Highland Seer. From that day to the moment of his passing, he guided me through the mysteries of Scottish witchcraft with quiet depth and unwavering presence. I was eager—always reaching for the following teaching, always wanting to go deeper—but Swein often touched my shoulder and said, "You must take your time, lass. In our tradition, you must learn for thirty years before even thinking of working the advanced." Those words were a lodestone in my soul. Back then, I didn't fully understand. Now I know: True magick is not rushed. It is remembered, endured, and embodied. Even after all these years, I am still learning. Each day reveals a new layer. Each spell cast teaches me something more. And that makes this chapter advanced—not complexity for its own sake, but the depth of lived gnosis that runs through every word.

These teachings are drawn from a lifetime of experience, walking the boundaries between worlds, warding sacred ground, and carrying the weight of protection for others. They are not simply spells. They are living tools, spirit forged and shadow tested. When your dreams grow louder, your presence begins to ripple through the unseen, and your energy stirs what lies beneath the land, you will know it is time. If you have found yourself called to these pages, then welcome. The circle opens to you now. Stand firm, walkwise. And remember, magickal practitioner: This is not the end of your learning, but the beginning of your becoming.

WHY THIS IS CONSIDERED ADVANCED MAGICKAL PROTECTION

There comes a point on your path where basic protection is no longer enough—when the deeper layers of magick begin to stir, and you realise that true defence isn't just about lighting sage or wearing a black stone. It's about sovereignty. It's about spirit. And it's about knowing who you are in every realm.

WHY I CONSIDER THIS ADVANCED

Here's why I call these practices advanced and what makes them so powerful.

- Because it works in the unseen: This level of protection moves through dimensions. It doesn't just stop bad vibes—it shields you from psychic attacks, energetic cords, astral interference, and dark projections.
- Because it demands focus and precision: You're no longer doing casual magick. You're working with layers, casting, invoking, sealing, and weaving intention with every breath.
- Because you're now interacting with external forces: You may be warding off envy, spellwork, entity attachments, or energetic parasites at this level. It's not just about your bubble anymore.
- Because there's responsibility involved: Some techniques—like mirror magick or banishments—affect the energetic field beyond you. You must use discernment and understand the ripple effect.
- Because it calls on higher powers: Whether you invoke deity, ancestors, elements, or sacred symbols, this work is rooted in ancient systems and must be done with reverence.

WHAT MAKES IT ADVANCED IN NATURE

Outside of my beliefs, here is why it is naturally more advanced work:

- Because it weaves multiple systems, these protections often combine sigils, rituals, spoken spells, planetary timing, crystal grids, herbs, and spirit allies—all in harmony.

- Because your will powers it, the herbs and tools don't do the work—you do. Your will, your command, and your spiritual strength seal the magick.
- Because it requires inner work, to be truly protected, you must face your shadows. What within you still allows harm? What have you yet to reclaim?
- Because you command space and spirit, you're not begging for safety—you're declaring sovereignty. You're stating, "This is my realm. No harm may enter."
- Because your craft becomes bespoke, this is no longer generic. Your protections become yours; handcrafted poppets, carved mirror wards, sacred seals, and spoken declarations are uniquely spoken in the language of your lineage.

WHEN YOU'RE READY TO BEGIN THIS WORK

To decide if you are ready to move into advanced work, review these tips:

- When your daily protections are strong and stable: If you cleanse regularly, ground deeply, and shield with intention, your field is solid and you're ready to build upon it.
- When you sense you're under psychic attack or influence: If you feel drained, targeted, or distorted by something outside yourself, advanced protection isn't a luxury; it's a necessity.

- When you hold space for others: Healers, teachers, mediums, and witches working with groups or clients must shield more powerfully to protect themselves and the people they serve.
- During spiritual thresholds: If you're undergoing a rite of passage, shadow work, an initiation, a past-life retrieval, or ceremonial work, you need deep layers of protection.
- When your spirit tells you: That quiet inner voice, those dreams, those moments of knowing—they whisper when it's time. Trust the call.

Let me share this wisdom with you: When you step into this level of work, you step into your true power. And once you do, you don't go back. This is where you stop reacting to harm and start commanding your space as the witch, the seer, the soul you came here to be.

THE WITCH'S COMPASS

In the heart of every wise person is a compass, a deep inner knowing that guides us through the seen and unseen worlds. It is not bound by north or south but by the energetic forces surrounding us. It spins in response to the pull of light and shadow, guiding us through energy-filled spaces. The following advanced occult practices will help heighten your awareness and unlock your ability to sense the energies that swirl around you.

This inner compass is more than a tool; it is an innate part of you as a magickal being. Trust it. This inner compass will become a powerful ally in your protection magick as you hone your awareness. It will guide you to where energy needs clearing, where your shields must rise, and where your power lies.

Protection begins with sensing, and your compass will always lead the way.

SACRED SILENCE

Your witch's compass finds its true north in silence. Keep your mind still and listen, for the unseen world speaks in quiet spaces. The energy around you will reveal itself when you are open to its whispers. Breathe deeply and let your compass guide you toward what is hidden beyond the mundane.

YOUR BODY AS THE COMPASS NEEDLE

Your body is the needle of the witch's compass, pointing toward disturbances or peace in the energy field around you. Please pay attention to the signals your body sends: a sudden chill, a tingling on your skin, or a wave of tension. These sensations are your compass aligning with the forces present. Trust your body to guide you, for it is finely tuned to the world of magick.

THE MOON AS GUARDIAN

The moon is the eternal guardian of the witch's compass. Under her light, your intuition sharpens, and your ability to sense energy heightens. When the moon is full, stand beneath her glow and let her guide your compass. Feel the energies around you respond and point you toward the disturbance if something feels off.

TRACING ENERGY WITH YOUR POWER FINGER

Let your power finger become the point of your compass. Walk the perimeter of your home or sacred space, tracing the air before you. Where the energy feels heavy or resistant, your compass guides you to areas needing protection. Mark these places as where your wards and spells must be cast.

THE THIRD EYE AND YOUR COMPASS

Close your physical eyes and open your psychic vision. Visualise the energy around you, feeling for shadows, colours, or shapes. As you train your third eye, your compass will grow stronger, revealing both light and dark forces in the spaces you inhabit. Trust your inner knowing and feelings.

DETERMINING THE PROTECTION NEEDED

When your compass is activated, it will guide you to the protection you need. Let it point you toward what requires attention. If the air feels heavy, your compass tells you to cleanse with salt, sage, or fire. If your body feels drained, your compass points to the need for psychic shields or protective crystals. If the energy feels chaotic, your compass urges you to place wards at your doors and windows. If you feel a dark presence, your compass calls upon the elements to banish what does not belong.

THE CAIM

There are moments in life that anchor us in understanding our power, moments when we realise that the unseen forces of protection are genuine and can be called upon at any time. For me, one of those moments was a journey I took with Swein Macdonald, the Highland Seer, up to a sacred site where the air seemed to hum with ancient energy.

Swein had been teaching me the ways of protection magick since I was young, and this journey was no different. As we walked toward the sacred site, he spoke of the ancient practice of the Caim. The Caim is a powerful and straightforward protection spell, a circle that can be drawn with the finger, invoking protection from all directions. It was not just a ritual but a way of acknowledging the presence of guardians, ancestors, and spirits of the land.

When we arrived, Swein instructed me to stand still, to feel the earth beneath my feet, and to draw a circle around myself with my finger, a silent but potent declaration of protection. As I did so, I could feel the energy shift, the air becoming thick with the presence of unseen forces. This simple act, this sacred circle drawing, was my first profound encounter with the power of protection magick in action. The circle I traced was not just a boundary of space but a shield that encompassed my body and spirit.

This is called the Caim. It comes from the ancient Celtic tradition and is a powerful yet straightforward act of magickal protection.

Swein spoke of how the Caim is not just a physical act but a calling upon the earth's and sky's energies to protect, a reminder that we are never alone. From that day forward, I knew that protection could be summoned with a simple gesture, a flicker of intent, and a connection to the ancient forces that have always surrounded us.

That day with Swein reinforced what I have since come to teach others: Protection is not something we wait for; it is something we create.

Creating a circle of protection with my own finger has become one of my most trusted methods. Whether I was faced with negative energies, psychic attacks, or just the need to feel safe, the Caim always stood as a reminder that protection is within my power. It doesn't require elaborate rituals or tools, just intention and belief in the magick that flows through us all.

Ritual: Calling the Circle of Protection

The Caim is a simple yet profound way to claim your space, to declare to the universe that your energy is your own, shielded and strong. Using your power finger, you channel your will into creating a shield of light around you.

This ritual reminds us that protection is accessible at any moment, rooted in intention and ancient practice, knowing that our ancestors walk beside us.

Needs

Your power finger; a natural, open space (forest, field, or near water); and a small token or offering for the land spirits.

Directions

Go to a place in nature where you feel connected to the elements. Stand barefoot if possible. Close your eyes, breathe deeply, and ground yourself, becoming aware of the earth beneath you and the sky above. Set your intention by focussing on what you are seeking protection from. Remember that intention clearly, knowing you will soon invoke a protective circle.

Using your power finger, trace a circle around yourself, moving clockwise. As you do, call upon the elements for protection by saying, "By the earth beneath, solid; by the sky above, where I belong; by fire within, fierce and bright; by the waters flowing with light." Feel the energy of the circle form around you. Then place your hand over your heart and say, "By the circle's power and ancient decree, it is sealed." Allow the circle to solidify, creating a shield of protection. Finally, take a deep breath, feel the circle's protective energy around you, and leave a token of gratitude if you've brought one.

THE GUARDIANS OF THE HIDDEN VEIL

In the deepest reaches of the occult mysteries, there are entities who are neither gods nor spirits in the conventional sense but guardians of the liminal spaces, protectors of the veils between worlds. They are known by many names; some whisper to them as gatekeepers, others as threshold watchers. They exist on the edges of existence, ensuring that cosmic balance remains and that the realms stay separate, untouched by forces that would otherwise corrupt or destroy.

When you invoke the guardians of the hidden veil, you call upon the most ancient entities, older than the gods, who uphold the natural order. They are the ones who witnessed the first breath of creation and who will remain at the end of all things.

Ritual: Binding the Thresholds of Reality

This ritual practice centres on creating an arcane seal, a symbol of ultimate protection that guards the boundaries between the worlds. The arcane seal protects your physical space and seals the spiritual and energetic thresholds where dark forces might cross.

Needs

A black cloak with a hood, a black veil to cover your head and face, parchment or black cloth (on which to draw the seal), bloodstone or obsidian (to anchor the ritual), dragon's blood ink (for drawing the seal), three black candles (representing the three veils: birth, death, and the unknown), incense of myrrh (*Commiphora myrrha*) and sandalwood (to purify and empower), and a key or sigil representing the guardians of the veil.

Directions

Begin by putting on your magick-charged cloak and black veil over your head and face and casting a circle around you, invoking the elements and calling upon your personal guardians. Place the three black candles at the east, west, and south points of your circle, leaving the north open as a doorway to the unseen. Light the myrrh and sandalwood incense, allowing the smoke to clear the way for the hidden forces to enter.

Next, use the dragon's blood ink to draw an ancient sigil or seal on your parchment or black cloth, a design that represents both protection and binding. The shape can be intuitive, but it should feel primordial, like it comes from a place beyond time. As you draw, chant, "By the veil, by the gate, I bind the dark; I seal my fate. No force shall cross, no harm befall, I call the ancient guardians one and all."

Hold the bloodstone or obsidian in your hand and turn toward north, the unknown and the unseen. Begin to chant with deep intent, calling forth the guardians of the hidden veil: "Guardians of the threshold, watchers of the night, keepers of the realms beyond mortal sight; by blood and flame, I call your might; stand with me, protect this rite." Sense their presence gathering around the edges of your circle, standing guard as they watch over the boundaries you are about to seal.

Take the key or sigil representing the guardians of the veil and place it in the centre of your drawn seal. As you do, focus all your intent on creating an unbreakable barrier between the worlds. Speak the following words with conviction: "By this key, by this sign, I seal the gate where dark aligns; let no force pass, let none intrude, the veil is sealed, my will imbued."

Now visualise a brilliant light surrounding the seal, forming a wall of energy that expands outward, pushing back any dark or harmful entities. See this seal anchoring itself in your physical space and at the crossroads of time and reality, sealing the thresholds between worlds.

Light the three black candles, symbolising the three veils: birth, death, and the unknown. As they burn, pour your energy into the seal, repeating the chant, "Veil of birth, veil of death, by the guardians' breath, no harm shall pass; sealed and bound by flame and stone, this arcane seal, forever grown." Allow the candles to burn down completely, focusing on the seal's permanent charge with protection.

Once the candles have burned down, take the bloodstone or obsidian and keep it close to the seal as a permanent protective anchor. Thank the guardians of the veil for their presence and protection, saying, "Guardians of the hidden realms, your watch is done; I thank you, now return to where your strength resides; with honour, I release this vow." Close your circle and allow the seal to remain in your sacred space, knowing it is now permanently imbued with the power to guard against any forces that might seek to harm or cross into your realm.

In this final act, you have sealed your own space and fortified the boundaries between the worlds. You now stand as a keeper of the veil, empowered to maintain the delicate balance between light and shadow. The arcane seal is your permanent shield, a mark of your dedication to protection for yourself and the greater cosmic balance. This is the final layer of protection, the ultimate safeguard against the forces that dwell beyond our reality. With this, you stand fully empowered, fortified against all that seeks to harm or disrupt your journey as a witch, an occultist, and a guardian of the sacred.

19
THE SHADOW MIRE

We live in a time when unseen forces shaping our world have become more tangible and pervasive. From psychic attacks and rampant divisions to the slow decline of our collective spiritual and emotional health, we are now standing at the edge of a new abyss, one where an ancient darkness has begun to rise again, far-reaching and consuming.

This force is not new, nor is it unknown to those who walk the path of witchcraft. It has existed since the birth of civilisation, lurking just beneath the surface, seeping into human consciousness, feeding off fear, hate, and division. This force has a name: Shadow Mire.

WHAT IS SHADOW MIRE?

Shadow Mire is not just an entity but an egregore, a destructive thoughtform created and fed by centuries of war, hatred, greed, and the darkest human impulses. It thrives in the collective unconscious, gathering strength from chaos and despair, expanding its reach whenever division and conflict reign supreme. Its presence is sticky, invasive, and parasitic. Once it touches a mind, it spreads its dark tendrils through fear, mistrust, and pain, causing emotional and spiritual decay.

Shadow Mire is more than a metaphor for these times; it is their energetic reality. The wars, pandemics, societal division, and global suffering we witness today are not just the byproduct of human actions alone but are also driven by the ancient force of Shadow Mire, which feeds off this chaos and grows stronger by the day.

This dark force operates through fear, division, and ignorance. It was there during the fall of great empires, present in the witch trials, and felt during times of great societal unrest. Shadow Mire slithers into the cracks of human consciousness, infiltrating governments, media, and social discourse, breeding hatred and mistrust. It seeks to divide us from ourselves and each other, weakening our collective light.

But as witches, as those who walk between the worlds, we are called to do more than witness. We are called to stand against it.

DEFEATING SHADOW MIRE

To understand Shadow Mire's power, we must first acknowledge that it cannot be fought through mundane means alone. It is an ancient force that requires an ancient response. The power of light, love, and protection alone will not be enough to sever its tendrils, as it thrives on the subtle chaos of even well-meaning intentions. Shadow Mire requires a deeper intervention that calls upon the most ancient cosmic forces.

The ancient ones, beings who existed long before the gods and goddesses known to us today, are the only entities with the knowledge, the cosmic authority, and the strength to stand against this malevolent egregore. They are the firstborn of the void, entities that have witnessed the rise of worlds and the collapse of empires. These watchers, primordial forces of balance, guard the secrets of the universe, protecting the delicate weave of reality from corruption.

The names I share with you come from my occult teacher, Ralph Harvey, who is now in the summerlands. They do not appear directly in any known ancient texts, like the Book of Enoch. They represent beings tied to ancient energies, shadowy forces, or divine protectors invoked in hidden or lost mystical traditions, older than formalised religious systems.

They originate from fragmented oral traditions, occult teachings, or lesser-known arcane orders that predate written scripture and organised religion.

These names come from realms of intuitive or visionary experiences rather than easily accessible historical texts. Their presence is found more through direct mystical encounters, invocation, or deep meditative exploration.

These entities or beings have been touched upon in certain grimoires, obscure writings, or in the hidden traditions of ancient mystical orders, making them difficult to trace to any single source. They tap into an ancient current of knowledge that transcends the commonly known pantheons of gods and goddesses.

ELOA, THE WEAVER OF TEARS

Eloa, born of the Creator's tears at dawn, is one of the first watchers. Her power lies in her understanding of light and shadow; she can transmute darkness into light. Eloa is a vital ally in the battle against Shadow Mire because she doesn't seek to destroy but to transform. Her tears are not of sorrow but of profound wisdom, understanding that darkness is not to be feared but transmuted. When you call upon Eloa, you invoke her gift of turning shadow into light, transforming fear into understanding, hatred into compassion, and despair into hope.

THAMIEL, THE DUAL-FACED GUARDIAN

Thamiel stands at the crossroads of creation and destruction. His two faces allow him to see the dual nature of all things: Light cannot exist without shadow, and shadow cannot be sustained without light. Thamiel's role in the battle against Shadow Mire is critical because he is the gatekeeper between realms, able to seal the darkness within its dimension and prevent invasion into the physical and spiritual worlds. By calling upon Thamiel, you invoke his ability to lock away the darkness, confining it to where it can no longer harm the innocent or spread its parasitic tendrils.

XHUL, THE VOID WEAVER

Xhul's power lies in his ability to weave and unweave the threads of reality. He understands the cosmic fabric, knowing where Shadow Mire has entangled itself into the web of existence. By working with Xhul, you can unravel the destructive energies, disentangling the web that Shadow Mire has woven around individuals, communities, and nations. Xhul allows you to protect yourself and unweave Shadow Mire's influence from your loved ones, home, and sacred spaces.

VOHU MANAH, KEEPER OF PURE THOUGHT

One of the most critical forces to invoke in this battle is Vohu Manah, the keeper of pure thought. His power is essential in protecting the mind from corruption. Shadow Mire thrives by infiltrating the collective psyche, feeding on fear and negativity. Vohu

Manah shields the mind, creating a barrier against the invasive thoughtforms Shadow Mire sends to weaken us. By calling upon Vohu Manah, you strengthen your and others' mental defences, ensuring that your thoughts remain your own, untainted by the fear and negativity Shadow Mire seeks to spread.

THE MOURNERS OF FORGOTTEN REALMS

The mourners are entities charged with sealing ancient evils into forgotten realms. They must ensure that destructive forces like Shadow Mire are banished from our dimension and locked away so they can no longer influence humanity. When invoked, the mourners can bind Shadow Mire and its tendrils, preventing it from further infecting the world. Their presence ensures the corruption is contained, sealing Shadow Mire within the deepest, most inaccessible realms, where it can no longer reach or feed on our fear and division.

Ritual: A Call to the Ancient Guardians

In this time of significant imbalance, we must not fear to call upon these beings. Though they are beyond the realm of gods and goddesses, their power is not destructive but restorative. They are the guardians of the cosmic balance, the weavers of existence, and they hold the key to dissolving the poisonous influence of Shadow Mire. This ritual will help you call upon these guardians.

Needs

Blackthorn wood or a branch (representing protective magick), a mirror (to reflect and return harmful energy), dragon's blood oil (for banishment and empowerment), a silver or black candle (symbolising the light piercing the shadow), a bowl of salt water or blackthorn salt (to purify and cleanse), and sigils of the ancient ones (carved or drawn on paper).

Directions

Cast a circle of protection around you using salt water, sprinkling it in a clockwise motion while speaking: "I cast this circle of protection by the powers of earth, air, fire, and water. No harm shall enter, and no darkness shall pass." Take the black or silver candle and anoint it with the dragon's blood oil, charging it to banish Shadow Mire and any dark influences surrounding you.

Hold the blackthorn branch in your hand and place the mirror before you. Light the candle and call upon the ancient ones: "By the firstborn of the void, by the light before the stars, Eloa, Thamiel, Xhul, I call you from afar. Vohu Manah, mourners of old, stand with me this hour; I ask for your guidance; lend me your power. Eloa, transmute the shadow into light. Thamiel, seal the darkness, keep it from sight. Xhul, weave the threads that Shadow Mire tore. Vohu Manah, protect my mind forevermore."

Visualise the candle's light expanding, pushing back the sticky tendrils of Shadow Mire. See the mirror reflecting the darkness to its source and feel the ancient power of the watchers standing guard, shielding you from parasitic energy. Allow the candle to burn down completely. As it does, take the sigils of the ancient ones and bury them under the earth or in a sacred space, symbolising their continuous protection.

20
MAINTAINING A DAILY PRACTICE

Protection is our constant companion from the dawn's first light to the shadows of the night. By incorporating morning, day, and night protection practices into our lives, we align ourselves with the natural energy cycles that surround and are within us. In our modern world, where energy can be easily disrupted by technology, stress, and the energy of others, these practices ground us and provide the coping mechanisms and breathing space we need to live better.

VISUALISATION

Visualisation is one of the witch's most powerful tools. By simply closing your eyes and weaving an image of protection, you can manifest a shimmering cloak of light that shields you from all harm. A daily visualisation routine can be incredibly potent at dawn or dusk when the veil between worlds is thin and our magick is strongest.

Sit quietly under the sky, whether it's the rising sun or the gentle glow of twilight. Close your eyes and see a brilliant light descending from above, wrapping around you like a soft, protective cloak. Whisper, "I am wrapped in the goddess's light; no harm may touch me, no shadow may find me. I am safe; I am whole." Imagine this cloak shimmering around you, reflecting any negative energy away as you walk in the light of your protection.

LAUGHTER MAGICK

Laughter has the power to break curses, dispel darkness, and raise a space's energy. Laughter is like a cleansing wind, blowing away the heaviness of fear, doubt, and negativity. Embracing laughter in your practice can turn even the darkest night into a time of joy and protection. Try lighting a yellow candle at the centre of your sacred space. Think of something that brings you pure joy, whether a memory, a loved one, or a funny moment. As you laugh, visualise the sound of your laughter as golden light flowing outward, banishing all negativity from your space. Now say, "By the joy in my heart, I cast out all fear; by the light of laughter, no darkness may draw near."

TENDING TO YOUR ENERGY

In the world of magick, your energy is your most sacred tool, a flame that burns brightly, protecting, guiding, and empowering you. But like any fire, it must be tended. Each day, the forces of the world, both seen and unseen, can dim or disturb this sacred flame. That's why it's essential to check in with your energy, to feel its pulse and presence. Strengthen it with the grounding of earth, the breath of air, the flow of water, and the fire within your spirit. Fortify it with boundaries and let your light shine strong and untouchable. This is your shield, your magick, and your power. Guard it well.

DAILY ENERGY CHECK-IN

Set aside a few moments each day, ideally in the morning and before bed, to do an energetic check-in. This is like a scan of your body, mind, and aura to see how you're feeling and whether there are any disturbances.

Sit or lie down in a quiet space where you won't be disturbed. Close your eyes and take deep breaths to calm your mind. Mentally scan your body, starting from your feet and working your way up to the crown of your head. Focus on any sensations, areas of tension, or discomfort. As you do this, pay attention to your emotions. Are you feeling anxious, drained, or unsettled? Or do you feel calm and grounded?

Visualise your aura, the energy field that surrounds you. Is it bright and expansive, or does it feel dim, cluttered, or heavy? Take note of any changes throughout the day. If your energy feels heavy after interacting with certain people or entering certain spaces, that's a signal of outside influence.

STRENGTHENING AND SEALING YOUR AURA

Your aura is your first line of defence against external energies, so keeping it strong and intact is essential. Here's a simple yet effective technique. Visualise a sphere of light surrounding you, about an arm's length away from your body. The light can be any colour that feels protective to you: White, gold, or violet are commonly used for this purpose.

See this light growing stronger, brighter, and more impenetrable. Imagine it as a shield that blocks out negativity, absorbing any external harm before it can reach you. Set your intention; say silently or aloud, "I strengthen my aura now. I am fully protected, and no negative energy can penetrate this shield." Reinforce this shield daily. The more you practice, the stronger your energetic field will become.

ENERGY CLEANSING RITUALS

Daily exposure to other people's energy and the stresses of life can weaken your personal energy field. Regular cleansing helps maintain clarity and balance. Here are some of the most effective methods:

- Energetic cord-cutting. Visualise any energetic cords between you and the person who drains your energy. Then, with intention, visualise cutting these cords with a sword of light. Say aloud or silently, "I release any energy that is not mine, and I reclaim my own energy." Use protective talismans. Carry or wear protective symbols or crystals, like an evil eye amulet or obsidian pendant, to block and deflect unwanted energy.
- Salt baths. Taking a ritual bath with sea salt or Epsom salts is incredibly purifying. As you soak, visualise the water drawing out negativity and replenishing your energy with purity and strength.
- Smoke cleansing. Use black smoke, herbs, or dragon's blood spray to cleanse your energy field. Waft the smoke around your body, starting from your feet and working upward. As you do this, set the intention that the smoke removes all negative, stagnant, or unwanted energies.
- Sound cleansing. Use drums, bells, chimes, or chanting to cleanse your aura and space. Sound's vibration

can dislodge stagnant energy and bring harmony back into your field.

TAKING RESPONSIBILITY FOR YOUR ENERGY

Becoming more self-aware and proactive is essential to ensure your energy is strong and fortified. Checking in with your energy field daily, cleansing regularly, grounding yourself, and setting clear boundaries will all help keep you protected from outside influences. The more you practice, the more sensitive and in tune you will become when your energy is affected, empowering you to take quick action and maintain your strength.

AFFIRMATIONS FOR PROTECTION

In the same way we craft spells and sigils, you can use affirmations to serve as protective incantations. These words are like verbal talismans, imbued with your personal magick and intent to protect you.

To create your affirmation, first identify your intention. What do you need protection from? Be specific, whether negative thoughts, psychic attacks, or harmful words.

Choose your words. Use words of power, such as *shield*, *protect*, *reflect*, and *cleanse*, to craft a statement that reflects your intent. Consider rhythm and repetition. Spoken words hold more power when chanted or repeated. Use a rhythm that feels natural to you and repeat the affirmation three times for emphasis. Use this affirmation daily or when you feel vulnerable to external energies or need to reaffirm your strength. Enchant your words with intention, and they will serve as a powerful shield in your daily practice.

I have included ten affirmations for you to try. Speak these affirmations daily and let the magick of protection weave through every aspect of your life. These affirmations will constantly remind you of your power, shielding you as you walk the path of the magickal and the unseen.

- I am protected by earth, air, fire, and sea. No harm shall come to me. Each element rises with me, shielding me with its ancient strength.
- I stand within my circle of power, and no ill can cross my sacred space. My energy is fortified and untouchable by those who seek to harm me.
- The light of protection shines around me, a radiant shield of magickal might. By the grace of the ancients, I walk safely, always guarded.
- No shadow can breach my spirit, for the unseen forces protect me. The old ones stand with me, the guardians of time and space.
- With every breath, I strengthen my aura, woven with spells of protection and light. I am encased in a veil of power, impenetrable to all malice.
- I invoke the ancient powers; by their decree, I am safe in body, mind, and soul. Their watchful eyes guard my path, protecting me from all harm.
- The magick within me grows stronger daily; I am the weaver of my protection. No curse, ill wish, or negative force can touch my sacred essence.
- I walk between worlds, unseen and shielded by the forces of the cosmos. The stars guide my steps, and the earth protects my body.

- By the moon's glow and the sun's rise, I cast a shield that no darkness can penetrate. Light and shadow bow to my command; I am sovereign in my protection.
- I am the keeper of my energy, and only love and light may enter my space. My heart is strong, my spirit is fierce, and my protection is eternal.

GROUNDING PRACTICES

Grounding is essential for staying connected to the earth and centred in your body. Without grounding, your energy can become scattered and vulnerable to external influences. The following are different ways to stay grounded.

- Earthing. Go outside and place your bare feet on the ground. Visualise roots growing from your feet deep into the earth, anchoring you. Feel the solid support of the earth beneath you, drawing up stability and strength.
- Grounding breath. Sit comfortably and focus on your breathing. Inhale deeply, imagining the energy from the earth rising through your feet into your body. Exhale and release any tension or negativity into the earth, where it can be neutralised.
- Using crystals. Carry grounding stones like black tourmaline, hematite, or smoky quartz with you to stay anchored and protected throughout the day.

MORNING AND EVENING PRACTICES

Each dawn offers a fresh beginning, but as the sun rises, so do the energies, seen and unseen, that can weave their way into your day. To walk through the world empowered and protected, a morning ritual is essential, aligning you with the forces of nature and shielding you from harm. Here are three powerful yet straightforward practices to weave protection magick into your mornings: These morning rituals, though simple, weave powerful magick into the start of your day. With the elements, the sun, and the earth's crystals by your side, you walk shielded in light and strength, ready to face whatever may come.

MORNING PROTECTION

As the sun rises, it symbolises new beginnings and renewal of energy. We, too, can greet the day with a protective morning ritual, harnessing the power of the sun's first rays to surround ourselves in light. When you wake, sit or stand at your altar or face the sun if possible. Light a gold or yellow candle and hold your hands up to greet the morning light. Speak these words aloud: "By the light of the rising sun, I call upon Ra, the radiant one. Shield me in your golden rays, guide me through these waking days. With each step I take, I walk in the light, protected by the sun, both day and night." Visualise a glowing sphere of light surrounding you, bright and warm. Carry this shield with you throughout your day, knowing that Ra's energy moves with you, protecting your path.

DAILY ELEMENTAL CLEANSING

Before stepping into the day, cleanse yourself with the elements that form the foundation of magick. Use earth to ground and absorb negativity; hold a stone or sprinkle salt around your feet. Invoke air by lighting incense, allowing its fragrant smoke to clear away lingering shadows. For fire, light a candle, visualising its flame, burning away any unwanted energies. Finally, bless yourself with water, whether by misting with a charged spray, rinsing your hands under flowing water, calling on its cleansing flow to wash away any lingering harm, or using a blackthorn salt scrub to cleanse your body in the shower.

EVENING PROTECTION

As the veil of night falls and the world quiets, our energies shift, becoming more vulnerable to the unseen forces that stir in the darkness. To ensure peaceful and protected rest, evening rituals fortify your energy for the Dreamtime ahead. Here are three sacred practices to incorporate into your nightly routine; by weaving this protective magick into your evening, you shield yourself from the unseen energies that move at night, ensuring that your spirit rests safely until dawn.

PROTECTIVE BATHS

Bathing is another way to cleanse yourself of unwanted energy. Fill a small cloth bag with dried rosemary, mugwort, basil, lavender, and St. John's wort, along with a dark crystal such as black tourmaline or smoky quartz. As you sink into the water, feel its warmth, which cleanses away the day's energy and purifies your spirit. Envision a shield of light wrapping around your body as you rise from the water, sealing in the protective magick for the night.

LUNAR SHIELDING

After cleansing in a bath or other ways, you can use the moon's glow to shield yourself and bathe your spirit. Under the moon's soft glow, step outside or gaze from a window, drawing down the lunar energy. Whisper your intention to the moon, asking her to guard your dreams and shield your subconscious from harm. As the moon's light touches you, envision a silver veil of protection wrapping around your mind, creating a sanctuary as you sleep.

Ritual: Nighttime Ritual of Protection

The night is a powerful time to recharge our energy, heal, and strengthen our spiritual defences. Creating a nighttime protective ritual ensures that our spirit is safe as we journey through Dreamtime and that any lingering energies from the day are dissolved.

Needs

Black and blue candles, a small bowl of water, and a protective oil such as frankincense or myrrh.

Directions

Before sleep, light a black candle for protection and a blue candle for peace. Place a small water bowl on your altar to symbolise the cleansing of the day's energy. Anoint your third eye with a protective oil to shield your dreams and connect with divine protection.

As you prepare to rest, say, "By the moon's light and the stars' gentle glow, I call on the guardians of the night below. Wrap me in the wings of the sacred sky, let no ill pass as I close my eye. Anubis, watch over my dreaming soul; Sekhmet, defend as the night winds roll. In this sacred circle, my soul is at rest; I am protected, guided, and blessed."

Feel the protective energy surround you like a soft, glowing veil. Visualise it, sealing your aura, creating a boundary that nothing harmful can cross. As you drift into sleep, you are guarded by the ancient energies, safe to explore the dream realms.

INCANTATIONS

Whether you're heading into a situation that feels energetically draining, dealing with difficult people, or simply seeking a shield from negative influences, speaking your protection into existence empowers you to take control of your energy. Here are some ideas:

- Speak a protective incantation as part of your morning ritual, asking Ra to guide you throughout the day and Heka to weave a magickal shield around you.
- Chant a nighttime incantation, asking the gods to watch over you while you rest, ensuring your dreams are protected from harm.
- In times of crisis, call upon your spoken words to push back against negative forces when you feel threatened or energetically attacked. The power of your voice can act as a sword, cutting through harmful energies.

It's essential to remember that the power of protection magick is not merely found in the tools or symbols we use, but in the words we speak. You are the vessel through which magick flows, and with each spoken word, you summon forth the forces of the divine. The incantation becomes your shield and voice, the key to unlocking your magickal defence.

REMEMBER TO PRACTICE

It's essential to be aware of how the energy around us interacts with our own world, full of distractions and chaotic vibrations. You must create boundaries that protect your personal power and use the techniques that I have shared. Whether dealing with difficult people, challenging environments, or simply the wear and tear of daily life, having energetic protection in place is crucial.

Remember to use verbal shields throughout the day; if you feel your energy waning or negativity creeping in, whisper words of power to reassert your protection. Say, "I am shielded by ancient might; no ill shall touch me, day or night."

Don't forget to cleanse your energy regularly. Use tools like a small rosemary sprig or a piece of black tourmaline to cleanse your energy field during the day as well. You can do this by holding the tool close to your body or by mentally pushing away any unwanted energies with intention.

These two practices alone can help fortify you as you navigate the day, creating a protective bubble around you to keep your energy intact and shielded. Many of these practices were mentioned in earlier chapters, and this list is a reminder to do them daily.

Conclusion

A WYRD AND WONDROUS WEB

In witchcraft, we are the weavers, actively shaping our destiny through the power of intent and magickal action. Cosmic systems of reward and punishment do not govern our practice, but rather a more profound understanding of wyrd—the ancient web of cause and effect, where every action, every spell, and every word sends ripples through the universe. Every spell we cast, every intention we set, is a thread added to this vast, ever-changing tapestry. The energy we send out does not return unchanged; it moves through the web, shifting and intertwining with the energies of others. It may return altered, magnified, or softened, carrying the echoes of the paths it crossed.

We are creators, spinners of destiny. Through the magick we weave, we guide the threads of our lives and the lives of others. Our power lies not in controlling the web but in understanding how to move within it, work with the forces of the universe, and weave our desires into the fabric of existence. Intent is the key. What energy are you weaving with your thoughts, words, and actions? What are you sending into the world, and how will it return to you?

We know that energy spirals through the web of existence, constantly interacting with other energies. What we send out may pass through darker forces or be uplifted by positive ones, but it will always return, shaped by the journey it took. With every spell we cast and every action we take, we weave ourselves deeper into the fabric of the universe. The web responds to us, and we are never separate from the energies we manipulate. If we send out harm, we must be prepared for that energy to return. If we send out healing and love, the web will reflect that to us in time.

Fate, in the eyes of the magickal practitioners, is not rigid. It is fluid, ever-changing, and shaped by the seen and unseen forces we work with. The Wyrd Sisters—Clotho, Lachesis, and Atropos—are the guardians of the loom, watching over the threads of destiny. However, even though they do not fully control the web, we have the power to influence what lies between the spinning and the cutting.

As we weave, so too are we woven. Every spell, every knot tied, every intention sent ripples through the web, shaping the tapestry of our lives and the lives of those connected to us. Magick is not about surrendering to fate; it's about stepping fully into your power, knowing that you are both a creator and a participant in the cosmic web of existence.

In the world of magick, protection is both an art and a necessity. From the stones beneath our feet to the feathers carried on the wind, every element of the natural world offers strength to guard against harm, negativity, and unwanted forces. You now hold a comprehensive guide to the powerful tools available; each item, whether a crystal, herb, feather, or symbol, carries centuries of magickal tradition and elemental power.

Remember that protection is not just about defence as you weave these items into your spells, rituals, and daily witchy practices. It's about creating a sacred space where your energy can thrive, shield you from harm, and manifest your intentions without interference. With this collection of sacred tools, you can face whatever comes your way, knowing that your magickal defences are as strong as the elements themselves.

Of course, there is always more to discover in the vast and mysterious world of magick. However, for now, this guide provides a powerful starting point, offering a foundational understanding of the protective forces you can call upon in your work. Trust in the energy of the earth, sky, fire, water, and spirit, and know that these tools will stand beside you as you walk your magickal path.

NOTES

NOTES

NOTES

TO WRITE TO THE AUTHOR

If you wish to contact the author or would like more information about this book, please write to the author in care of Llewellyn Worldwide Ltd. and we will forward your request. Both the author and the publisher appreciate hearing from you and learning of your enjoyment of this book and how it has helped you. Llewellyn Worldwide Ltd. cannot guarantee that every letter written to the author can be answered, but all will be forwarded. Please write to:

Barbara Meiklejohn-Free
℅ Llewellyn Worldwide
2143 Wooddale Drive
Woodbury, MN 55125-2989

Please enclose a self-addressed stamped envelope for reply, or $1.00 to cover costs. If outside the U.S.A., enclose an international postal reply coupon.

Many of Llewellyn's authors have websites with additional information and resources. For more information, please visit our website at https://www.llewellyn.com.